*E*mpowerment Takes More Than a Minute

*E*mpowerment
Takes More
Than a
Minute

Ken Blanchard
John P. Carlos & Alan Randolph

Berrett-Koehler Publishers
San Francisco

Berrett-Koehler Publishers, Inc.
155 Montgomery Street
San Francisco, CA 94104-4109
Tel: (415) 288-0260 Fax: (415) 362-2512

Ordering Information

Individual sales. Berrett-Koehler publications are available through most bookstores. They can also be ordered directly from Berrett-Koehler at the address above.

Quantity sales. Special discounts are available on quantity purchases by corporations, associations, and others. For details, contact the "Special Sales Department" at the Berrett-Koehler address above.

Order for college textbook/course adoption use. Please contact Berrett-Koehler Publishers at the address above.

Orders by U.S. trade bookstores and wholesalers. Please contact Publishers Group West, 4065 Hollis Street, Box 8843, Emeryville, CA 94662. Tel; (510) 658-3453; 1-800-788-3123. Fax: (510) 658-1834.

Printed in the United States of America

 Printed on acid-free and recycled paper that is composed of 50% recovered fiber, including 10% post-consumer waste.

Publisher's Cataloging-in-Publication Data

Blanchard, Kenneth H.

Empowerment takes more than a minute/ Ken Blanchard, John P. Carlos, Alan Randolph

p. cm.

ISBN: 1:881052-83-4

1. Management 2. Business I. Carlos, John P. II. Randolph, W. Alan. III. Title.

HD31.B53 1995   658

QB194-21301

First Edition

99 98 96   10 9 8 7 6 5 4

Dedication

to . . .

Dorothy Blanchard
Donald L. and Isabella Carlos
Wallace Randolph

who taught us so much about being empowered

F ew changes in business have been so well received yet so problematic as the movement to create empowered, employee-driven work environments. Empowerment offers the potential for tapping into a wellspring of underutilized human capacity that must be harnessed if organizations are to survive in today's increasingly complex and dynamic world.

Empowered employees benefit the organization and themselves. They have a greater sense of purpose in their jobs and lives, and their involvement translates directly into continuous improvement in the workplace systems and processes. In an empowered organization, employees bring their best ideas and initiatives to the workplace with a sense of excitement, ownership, and pride. In addition, they act with responsibility and put the best interests of the organization first.

The traditional management model of the manager in control and employees under control is no longer effective. To create an empowered workplace, management's role in organizations must move from a command-and-control mind-set to a responsibility-oriented and supportive environment in which all employees have the opportunity to do their best.

Shifting to an empowerment philosophy calls for changes in most aspects of an organization. Both managers and employees must learn, first, not to be bureaucratic and second, to be empowered. Unfortunately, many managers do not understand that empowerment involves releasing the power people already have, nor do they understand how to navigate the journey to empowerment.

Empowerment Takes More Than a Minute is a how-to book that guides readers step-by-step through one manager's struggle to discover the three essential keys to empowerment. By following the manager's odyssey to the Land of Empowerment, readers discover that they can take the same journey, which, like any heroic journey, is filled with paradox, challenge, and fitful stops and starts. *Empowerment Takes More Than a Minute* provides practical and simple concepts that CEOs, COOs, and managers at all levels in organizations both public and private can apply to their particular situations.

Though many managers have dismissed empowerment as another passing gimmick, we find that people in organizations are naturally attracted to the idea of enhanced involvement at all levels.

Also, we personally have seen organizations succeed
with empowerment. Since the mid 1980s, we have
worked extensively with a wide variety of companies
that were trying to create empowered workplaces.
These companies have taught us a great deal about
what empowerment is and how to create it. They
haven't always known the answers to the questions
raised by empowerment, and neither have we. Quite
the contrary, it has been through missteps that we
have learned the three keys to empowerment
presented in this book.

Empowerment is definitely achievable, but the
journey is not for the weak in spirit. For those of you
who undertake it, we urge you to stay the course. We
know that your path can be made easier if you start
with and stick to the three keys of empowerment
explained in *Empowerment Takes More Than a Minute.*

Good luck on your journey.

Ken Blanchard   *John Carlos*   *Alan Randolph*

Fall 1995

Table of Contents

$\mathbf{T}$he rain beat down steadily. Occasionally the wind threw great splashes against the executive office windows. The sound brought a smile to Marvin Pitts' face. It made him reflect on the beating he felt he was taking lately as president and CEO of a midsize, once-successful company.

Marvin had taken over leadership a little over a year ago, and he had instinctively done his usual thing— seize the checkbook and centralize all decision making. He had developed quite a reputation as a "turnaround" manager and in the process had decided that lack of leadership at the top was usually the cause of a company's problems. As a hands-on manager, it didn't take him long to address that void. Nonetheless, he was beginning to notice that his old ways didn't seem to be working.

Another sheet of rain blasted the office windows, rousing Marvin from his trance. He looked up at the sign on his desk given to him by the consultant his board had recommended for hire.

The sign was really starting to bother him, but he
didn't have the nerve to take it down. It read:

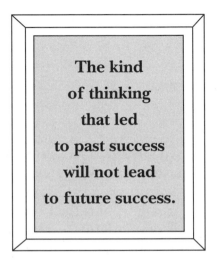

He recalled the consultant putting the sign there
after giving Marvin and his management team the
results of a study conducted on their industry, their
competition, and the company itself. It was there to
remind Marvin and others of a painfully obvious fact
that the study had confirmed—*management's thinking
is the first thing that has to change.*

The board had insisted that Marvin use this
consultant, because they felt the "world of business
lately" was changing so rapidly that he could no
longer figure everything out alone. They felt he
needed help. Marvin didn't agree, yet he had to
admit that the consultant's study did bring up some
interesting points.

In no uncertain terms, the study warned that the company would be outstripped by its competition unless all thinking, structure, processes, and action conformed to four critical organizational attributes. The company needed to be:

1. Customer-driven

2. Cost-effective

3. Fast and flexible

4. Continually improving

Now, as he had so many times before, Marvin mentally reviewed each item on that list.

1. Customer-driven

No one needed to convince Marvin that in today's market, success begins with customers. Still, he missed the old "buyer beware" days when mass-produced products were sure to be consumed, competition was moderate and primarily local, and customers had few choices. Yet, change had come with blinding speed. With the sophistication of today's customers and the variety of products available, the study insisted that any organization not responsive to customers' wants and needs was doomed to be second rate or soon out of business!

2. Cost-effective

The importance of this attribute didn't surprise Marvin, either. Cost increases, together with fierce pricing battles with competitors, had forced companies to shave margins to a fraction of what they had been. Now was clearly a time in which companies were forced to do far more with far less in order to survive.

3. Fast and flexible

The third attribute always brought a moan from Marvin. It pointed in precisely the opposite direction from what he had been accustomed to and comfortable with in the past. He had liked the old paradigm where decision making drifted up the hierarchy. It gave him a chance to get his arms around problems.

However, the study pointed out that changing customer needs had made the cumbersome layers of bureaucratic management as deadly as high cholesterol levels. In the time it took business decisions to move up the hierarchy and back down again, the customer would be long gone. These days, buyers no longer cared who Marvin Pitts was—nor about anyone else at the top of the organization. It was the frontline people they dealt with who made the difference. Marvin bemoaned how sad that was, yet he knew it was true.

Customers wanted their contacts in the company—frontline employees—to make decisions, solve problems, and take action right on the spot. Clearly, quicker was better, and Marvin was reluctantly beginning to accept that point.

4. Continually improving

Everywhere Marvin turned, he heard that lifelong learning had to become a norm in his company. Everyone in the company would have to embrace the vision of a corporation that would be better today than it was yesterday and better tomorrow than today. Marvin knew that would be a difficult task—creating an organization that would steadily and consistently outdo itself.

Remembering all this, Marvin took a deep breath and then slowly and dramatically released it. Consultants, consultants, consultants, he thought. It's easy for them to make recommendations. But who has to do the work of implementing their ideas? Me!

Once he calmed down, Marvin realized the consultant's recommendations were right. He knew that if the company were to survive, he would have to create an organization that was *customer-driven, cost-effective, fast and flexible,* and *continually improving.* But how?

The advice kept coming back from everyone: *We've got to become leaner and meaner, with fewer management layers.*

We have to release all the untapped creative energy in the company. People must be invited to take responsibility and make full use of their skills and abilities. Everyone needs to feel *empowered* to carry out the charge of making the company more responsive to customers and at the same time financially sound.

Empowerment, thought Marvin. He had begun to hate that word. That's all people talk about today, particularly consultants, and now my board has the disease, he moaned to himself. It used to be that people were happy just to have a job. Now they want more than a job, they want a fulfilling job—one that makes them feel like they are making a real contribution.

Under pressure, Marvin had already made one significant reduction in the work force and eliminated two layers of management. If they want a lean and mean company, he had reasoned, I'll give it to them!

That was nine months ago, Marvin mused, yet nothing seems any different. As he looked out at the driving rain he wondered, where is the spirit of responsibility at work? Where is all that desire to make a contribution?

The sad truth was that throughout the organization people were acting no differently than they had when the company was a multilayered bureaucracy. No one in this new "leaner and meaner" company seemed willing to step up to the plate and take on the challenge. A pall of reluctance hung over the workplace.

6

As Marvin took the pulse of the company—meeting with employee groups, visiting the shop floor, asking questions of the front line—he had yet to see people *acting* empowered. In fact, they went about their business in the same manner as when the company was dominated by its deadly bureaucratic mind-set. With all the talk about the need for empowerment, Marvin thought the shift would happen spontaneously once the place had been downsized. Obviously, that was not the case.

Everywhere Marvin looked, employees' faces were masks of denial. He sensed that to them, the word *empowerment* was just that, a word—the *E* word. It was driving him crazy!

He often thought of the old maxim, "The more things change, the more they stay the same," and it made him cringe. I knew it, he would say to himself, empowerment is just another buzzword.

Marvin studied an article laying on his desk. In spite of his recent skepticism, this particular article intrigued him. The author insisted that empowerment works, and that it just takes more than a minute to get there. The article stated you can't tell people to act empowered and expect them to just do it. If they have no past experience or involvement in decision making, they won't know what to do.

Citing an example of a company's success in empowering its people, the article went on to rave about the turnaround of a textile manufacturing and distribution company that had been caught napping by the advent of the new information economy. The manager, some guy named Sandy Fitzwilliam, was credited with having an incredibly motivated staff who acted as if they owned the company. In fact, the article referred to Fitzwilliam as "the Empowering Manager."

Maybe I ought to talk to him, thought Marvin. Most of the consultants I've met over the years have never actually managed anything themselves. Maybe I can talk with this Fitzwilliam guy in practical terms, man to man.

It seemed like a good idea, yet Marvin was reluctant as he dialed information for Fitzwilliam's number. He always hated to admit he needed help. It drove his wife crazy that he would never stop to get directions when they were lost. He would drive around stubbornly trying to figure out how to get to their destination on his own. Only as a last resort would he stop and ask for help.

I guess this is one of those "last resort" times, Marvin thought to himself. My board is not going to want to wait forever while I figure out how to make this company profitable again.

With that thought as his motivation, Marvin dialed the Empowering Manager's number. After two rings, he was greeted by a woman's voice saying, "Hello!"

"I'd like to speak with Mr. Fitzwilliam, " Marvin requested.

"Speaking," was the quick reply.

Marvin was caught completely off guard. It never even entered his mind that Fitzwilliam could be a woman. Empowerment was a tough enough concept for him to swallow as it was, and now to find out that Sandy Fitzwilliam is a woman!

This feels like piling on, thought Marvin. I can't believe it. The so-called Empowering Manager is a woman! And on top of it all, she answers her own phone!

Sandy Fitzwilliam broke the silence by asking, "Hello, are you still there?"

"Yes. Yes," stammered Marvin.

"What can I do for you?" she asked politely.

Marvin's mind was racing a mile a minute. Even though he was uncomfortable asking for help and desperately wanted to hang up, he found himself reluctantly explaining his situation and his need for some advice.

"We've streamlined our company so people can take more initiative and respond to customers more quickly. But people are still sending decisions back up the hierarchical ladder. I've talked a lot about empowerment, and I can't understand why—"

"What exactly is the problem?" the Empowering Manager interrupted.

Marvin gulped and thought for a moment. Then he said simply, "People won't run with the ball."

"Let me ask you something," she began. "Have you ever arrived at a store one minute after closing time, only to find the door locked? You needed something badly, and you saw people inside, so you knocked on the door—and nobody even looked up."

"Yes. That happened to me just last week!" Marvin exclaimed.

"Whose fault did you think it was? Who did you blame as you drove away?"

"The employees, of course!" Marvin answered. "I bet the manager wasn't even there, and the workers were watching the clock, anxious to close shop. They probably weren't even thinking about me. They just wanted to get the heck out of there."

"Wrong!" Fitzwilliam chimed.

"What do you mean, wrong?" Marvin asked defensively.

"Of course the employees were anxious to leave. But you're wrong about who was to blame. The fault was the owner's. Whoever the owner is, he or she did nothing to make the people who work there feel like they own the business. Otherwise, they would have opened the door."

Marvin thought it over in silence.

"Let me ask you another question," the Empowering Manager went on. "If people were given the option, do you think they'd choose to be magnificent or ordinary at work?"

"Magnificent."

"Do you really believe that? Or are you just saying it because you think you should believe it?"

"Why would you ask that?" Marvin inquired.

"Because I don't have a lot of time here. I need to know about your real, honest-to-goodness, core beliefs. If you don't have a basic faith in people, it's time for us to hang up."

Marvin was taken aback. Wow, he thought, this woman docsn't beat around the bush at all.

He answered reluctantly, "Well, if you must know, I don't have that much faith in people. It's partly because of the old hierarchical thinking I grew up with and is something I've been striving to overcome. When I think about it, it makes sense that people would rather do their best at their jobs, given the choice. But that's when I think about it. My gut instinct is that people are not that responsible."

"I appreciate your honesty," the Empowering Manager replied. "Recognizing that the world might pass you by if you don't change is half the battle. This is particularly true when you understand what empowerment is and what it is not."

"That would certainly help," said Marvin. "I've never actually heard a good definition."

"Empowerment is *not* giving people power," she explained. "People already have plenty of power—in the wealth of their knowledge and motivation—to do their jobs magnificently. We define empowerment as letting this power out. But you see," she added in a more subdued tone, "I've learned this the hard way."

"Empowerment has a sense of ownership at its core, and it starts with the belief system of top management. Too many leaders still need to get over the notion that their people head off to work every morning asking themselves how they can get by with doing as little as possible today."

"When you put it that way, it sounds terrible," said Marvin. "Are there that many leaders who have so little trust?"

"I can only go by their behavior," said the Empowering Manager, "and by the results they get from their employees. It's not that people in organizations are unable to be their best—they're afraid to be their best. Most organizations are set up to catch people doing things wrong rather than to reward them for doing things right."

Marvin thought about that. "You know," he said, "I agree. I've seen organizations like that." Then he paused, sunk deep into thought, and finally said, "That's part of the problem at my company." Again he paused, then added, "But I'm not going to be that kind of leader anymore. If we are to be competitive, our company has to be a place where people are glad to show what they can do!"

"I think you're sincere," she said, "and I sense that your real satisfaction will come when you see your people taking charge. I also pick up on your hunger for winning. You obviously don't want to settle for being ordinary. But I need to remind you that empowerment is a top-down, values-driven issue. That's why I had to check out your values."

"So I passed, huh?" Marvin said sheepishly.

"For now. Can you come by my office at 2 P.M. this coming Tuesday?"

Marvin quickly glanced at his calendar and said, "Sure. I'll see you on Tuesday."

Just before she hung up, the Empowering Manager added, "We'll see if we can get you and your company started down the road to the Land of Empowerment."

Shortly before two o'clock the following Tuesday afternoon, Marvin pulled his car into the parking lot at Sandy Fitzwilliam's company and turned off the engine. From the passenger seat he picked up his notebook, opened the cover, and looked at the summary statement on the first page. He had written it there after his phone conversation with the Empowering Manager:

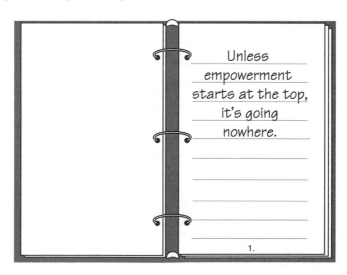

Unless empowerment starts at the top, it's going nowhere.

1.

"You can go right in," smiled the woman at the desk outside Sandy Fitzwilliam's office.

Marvin found the Empowering Manager standing by the window looking out. She turned and greeted him with a firm handshake. "I'm Sandy Fitzwilliam. Nice to meet you."

"Thank you for taking time to see me," Marvin began.

"Don't get too excited until you find out whether or not I can help you. Do you recall what I said as we hung up last week?" Sandy asked seriously.

Marvin thought for a minute. "Frankly, no."

"I told you that you were starting a journey."

"Oh yes," said Marvin. "Something about a journey to the Land of Empowerment. Sounds more like a ride at Disney World than anything else. I honestly don't know what you mean by it."

"It's not a fantasyland," she clarified. "It's real. What do you think it might mean?"

"Well," said Marvin, letting his mind roam, "the word *journey* suggests that it might take some time to get there."

Sandy nodded.

Encouraged, Marvin went on. "It also conjures up tales of adventure, where one follows roads that lead over steep mountains and through dark forests. Unexpected things happen. There are lots of tests along the way. Something like that."

"Very good," she nodded. "And, what about the phrase *Land of Empowerment?*"

"Sounds like a land different from the one where I'm living now, that's for sure—one where the customs of the inhabitants are not the ones I was raised with. It's foreign."

"You've done well," Sandy said, smiling with obvious satisfaction. "Even though you resisted the concept at first, it feels like you've grasped the main ideas, the time it takes, and the degree of difficulty. I particularly like the fact that you think of the Land of Empowerment as being foreign. Most of us who try to empower others get in our own way because of our traditional thinking."

"But come on, now—is it really that hard?" asked Marvin.

Sandy just stared at him with no reply, so he added, "Well, there's my answer. I wouldn't have come here if I'd had an easy time of it. I was hoping you could just hand me a ready-made formula."

Sandy smiled. "I'd be doing you a disservice if I gave you a pep talk about empowering people, handed you a set of rules, and said, 'Go do it.' As you've already learned, you may want your people to take the initiative, but at first they may not be able to act empowered. This shouldn't be surprising. To use your analogy of a foreign land, they don't yet know the language or the customs of the Land of Empowerment."

Marvin nodded as he began scribbling in his notebook.

"And neither do you."

Marvin looked up from his notes, and Sandy continued, "You and your managers may not yet be ready to deal with an empowered work force. It means learning a whole new way to manage— managing projects and cross-functional teams rather than work groups.

"Remember what I told you on the phone: Empowerment is not giving people power—they already have it!"

As Marvin nodded, Sandy pointed to a large plaque on her wall:

People already have power through their knowledge and motivation.

Empowerment is letting this power out!

Marvin's solemn look told her that he was mulling this over.

"Whatever happens, it's going to take time for you to get to the Land of Empowerment, and this journey is going to test you and others in your organization time and time again. You'll be impatient because of the lack of quick results, and you'll suffer setbacks.

"You or your associates will question why you ever started or whether your destination is worth it. The only thing that will keep you going is a huge amount of faith and trust in the journey."

She continued, "Have you ever tried to put into action something you believed deeply in, only to find out later that you'd been going about it all wrong?"

"Quite a few times," Marvin admitted.

"You'll have that same experience with empowerment. You've come here because what you've tried to do so far to empower people in your organization hasn't worked. So the question now is, 'Are you willing to let go of what you still think is true about it?'"

Marvin pondered the question. "Yes," he said, "if I understand what you mean."

"My own experience," Sandy said, "and that of others, suggests that this journey will be a series of discoveries. One of those discoveries may be that the path you have chosen won't get you there. The energy and intention you've devoted to empowering people may have to be rechanneled."

"That's what you mean when you say that I have to have trust in the journey itself?" questioned Marvin.

"Exactly."

"Okay, I'm beginning to get it," said Marvin. "I see that empowerment is not going to happen suddenly; I'm going to have to hang in there. But how will we know if we're making any progress along the way? My board will want to know that for sure."

"That's tricky, too. In the early stages, gains will be small. Yet it's important to keep an eye out for them and celebrate every one. You see, the nature of success itself has changed. There used to be clear signposts, but in these times of turmoil, managers can no longer count on the traditional benchmarks for success."

"Sounds like I'm going to have to convince my board that although it may be difficult to know we're getting there, it's not impossible to measure progress. We'll just have to find a new way to look for the signs," Marvin ventured.

"That's exactly right," Sandy said. "And there are other, less obvious payoffs that are significant and long-lasting. An example is the feeling of ownership that comes over people in an empowered culture. If you're open and receptive, even the times when you seem sidetracked will yield important findings. Also, right in the midst of all that frustration, you'll learn that you are being changed into an empowering person. It's as if the journey and the destination are one and the same."

"That sounds great," said Marvin, "but being empowered as a manager isn't very exciting if you're wondering about what you will be doing once the work force becomes empowered. To be honest with you, my contemporary managers and I fear that empowering the work force will lead not only to loss of power and control but to loss of jobs as well."

Sandy nodded, acknowledging her appreciation for Marvin's concern.

"I understand that's a fear," Sandy replied, "and it's a common one. When I first got into empowerment I was also fearful of losing my job, until I realized that you don't lose your job from empowering people; you just get a different one. Rather than directing, controlling, and supervising your people like in the old days, you serve as a linking pin between your people and the rest of the organization."

"What do you mean by linking pin?" puzzled Marvin.

Sandy explained, "Your new role as an empowering manager is coordinating efforts, acquiring resources, strategic planning, working with customers, coaching people, and the like. Everything you do is to help your people be more effective. Now you work for them rather than them working for you."

The two leaders sat quietly deep in thought. This was obviously an important issue.

Finally, Sandy broke the silence. "Trust me. This new role will become clear to you as you learn more about empowerment."

"Okay—for now," smiled Marvin.

"Are you ready, then, to begin the journey to the Land of Empowerment?"

"As ready as I'll ever be," replied Marvin. "Where do I start?"

Sandy pointed in the direction of her office door and said, "You have to start out there, with my colleagues in this organization."

"Your colleagues?" Marvin repeated.

Sandy nodded. "The people I work with in this organization, no matter what position they may occupy, are my colleagues, my associates, my partners. If I create an environment that allows them to make this a great organization, they have the potential every day, through their every action, to make that happen. So they are the real source of the information you seek—not me." With that, she stood up and ushered Marvin out the door.

Marvin found himself standing outside the office, bewildered. He walked over to the woman who had shown him in. "I'm Marvin Pitts," he said.

"I know," smiled the woman.

"Are you Ms. Fitzwilliam's secretary?"

"Actually, I'm her associate," came the reply.

Marvin found himself thinking, how did I know she was going to say that?

Then the woman added, "My name is Amelia Engel. How may I help you?"

"I want to find out about how empowerment works around here. So I guess I'd like to talk to some of your, um, associates."

"We're all involved in making this an empowered organization," replied Amelia, "so anyone here could help you."

"Perhaps I should start at the bottom. That's where empowerment really has to go, isn't it?"

"Not really," smiled Amelia. "Anyone who interacts with our customers is considered to be at the top."

"Okay, okay," laughed Marvin. "Then maybe I should start at the top."

"Let me suggest that you talk to Robert Borders in our Billing Services Department," said Amelia, picking up the phone. "They've made tremendous progress in the last year by reducing billing errors by 37 percent and response time to customer billing inquiries by 50 percent. I'll see if Robert is available."

A short time later, Marvin found his way to the billing response center, where Robert had suggested they meet.

He was surprised that it appeared to be a standard operation, with the same kinds of equipment his own company used. The people looked the same, too. But at this point he didn't know what to expect.

A young man approached him. "Hi, I'm Robert Borders. You must be the executive Amelia called me about. What can I do for you?"

"I just finished talking with Sandy Fitzwilliam, and now I need to talk with some associates in your company about empowerment. But even though empowering people is my goal, I'm skeptical. I've tried to institute empowerment with my associates, and, frankly, I haven't seen much change."

"How long have you been at it?" Robert asked.

"Nine months," said Marvin.

Robert nodded. "All people have doubts at the beginning. But that shouldn't be surprising. They're being asked to buy into something on faith. Not only have they had no experience with being empowered, in many cases they've been unempowered. Also in the beginning they don't know how the process is going to work. They have no sense of WIIFM."

"What's WIIFM?"

"What's-In-It-For-Me. You can't blame people for being skeptical. Enough flavor-of-the-month programs have come and gone for people to believe that this is just another one of them. That was certainly the attitude here."

"In fact, when Sandy started telling us that her goal was to build an organization of colleagues where everybody's potential would be used, we thought she'd lost her mind."

"Hmm," Marvin mused. "That could explain why people aren't acting empowered in my company. Beliefs change slowly, huh?"

"It takes time. At first, we didn't believe Sandy knew what she was talking about. But now, we know she was right," Robert added. "And it's not just that people feel better. We're much more effective and efficient than we were before. We feel better about ourselves, our leaders, and our company. We feel a real sense of ownership and empowerment."

"Well, talk is cheap," Marvin said, impatiently. He was irritated by the obvious satisfaction Robert felt with his department. Then he asked, "How did you get where you are today? Something must have happened to release all that energy. It didn't just—"

"Information," interrupted Robert.

"Information?" Marvin echoed.

"Yes," said Robert, "Information about how the business is doing—profits, scrap, budgets, market share, productivity, defects, and so on."

Robert took a laminated card out of his shirt pocket and handed it to Marvin:

> *The first key*
> *is to*
> *share information*
> *with everyone.*

"I don't get it," said Marvin. "Share information about company performance throughout the organization? That sounds like it could lead to chaos or anarchy. I can't imagine doing that in my company. And further, I think that many others would be very uncomfortable doing it."

"Then you can't create an empowered organization," replied Robert. He paused for emphasis, then said, "I'm going to tell you something. I know you're a CEO, a president and all, and perhaps if I didn't have Sandy as an example I'd hesitate to say this because of respect for your position. But that's the trouble right there—the perceived difference in people's positions that hangs over from the old hierarchical days. That perceived division between 'superior' and 'subordinate' is no longer very useful in business organizations. In fact, it works directly counter to success. Success today depends on team effort." Robert paused.

Marvin crossed his arms and just looked at Robert. This conversation is just not very helpful, he thought to himself. But after a few more moments of silence, he nodded for Robert to continue.

"You can walk out of here," said Robert slowly, never taking his eyes off Marvin. "You can deny what I'm saying until you're blue in the face. But the fact remains that those leaders who are unwilling to share information with their people will never have their people as partners in running the company successfully and will never have an empowered organization. This act of sharing information is absolutely crucial to empowering an organization. That's why it's the first key."

"You're asking for a major shift in thinking—almost a lobotomy," said Marvin with an uncomfortable laugh.

"I know it," said Robert. "Every leader has to fight the battle against habit and tradition in the depths of his or her own heart. Each leader has to make a leap of faith. The most crucial place the shift has to occur is inside you."

"It certainly would be a big first step for me," said Marvin emphatically.

"And why wouldn't it be?" asked Robert. "You happen to be one of those managers who's caught in what we call the 'big left turn.'"

"What's the big left turn?"

"It's the huge, all-encompassing collapse of traditional boundaries that's taking place due to the sudden explosion of information. Information is bringing down walls all over the world. It's happening in all of our institutions at once, and it can be very scary.

"Communication barriers like the Iron Curtain, the Berlin Wall, and apartheid began to crumble long before anyone made the collapse official. Why? The flow of information could not be controlled any longer, no matter how hard anyone tried."

"Like an old metal ice cube tray," Marvin mused, "that you've just filled with water. All the little square compartments of water are separate. Then suddenly someone reaches in and takes away the divider—"

"And all the water flows together into one. Excellent analogy," said Robert. "This is what's happening, and for leaders like you and me who have been raised in a different tradition, it's difficult to do something like share all the information with everybody. It takes courage. But don't wait around for it to feel good to you. Just take a leap of faith and *do it.* It'll feel good later on."

"Just do it," Marvin repeated. "But what about privileged information?"

"What do you mean by 'privileged information'?" asked Robert.

"You know—guarded information; known to a few; only certain people have it; sensitive," explained Marvin.

"How would you feel if you were one of the people on the 'outside' who was not privy to the privileged information, particularly when you knew the information was only a computer key away?" asked Robert.

That caught Marvin off guard. He hesitated for a moment and then smiled. "I'd feel pretty ticked off and left out, among other things."

"I bet you would," laughed Robert. "Withholding information carries all kinds of messages. It makes people think, 'I'm not in the know. They don't trust me. They think I'd do bad things with the information if I knew it. They think I'm too dumb to understand it,' and so forth."

"People don't feel trusted," Marvin reiterated. He was starting to get the importance of sharing information.

Robert nodded. "On the other hand, there's no better way to show people that you trust them than to share sensitive information. Information about this company used to be private and unavailable to most of us. When Sandy began sharing performance information, she sent a very strong signal to everyone that she trusted us; that she wanted us to use our knowledge and talents."

"So you're saying that trust is crucial for an empowered organization."

Robert nodded enthusiastically. "And if people throughout the organization don't feel trusted, effective decision making grinds to a halt. People don't feel empowered, and therefore they don't act empowered. You see:

People without information cannot act responsibly.

People with information are compelled to act responsibly."

"That's beginning to make sense to me," muttered Marvin.

"It's the heart of the matter," said Robert.

"People without information cannot monitor themselves or make sound decisions. People with information can."

Marvin began thinking about his own organization. He realized that people at his company did not have the information to really understand the business and its performance results. Nor did they operate with a basic sense of trust. He also realized that sharing privileged information, like Sandy did with her associates, could help people be more responsible and start them on the road to building trust.

As he was thinking, Marvin suddenly got a blinding flash of the obvious. He scribbled something in his notebook and then looked Robert squarely in the eye. "Of course! What you're saying is that information is the *currency* for responsibility and trust in the Land of Empowerment."

Robert smiled and nodded. "Every leader wants responsible and trustworthy people in the organization. But stop and think: How do you go about developing responsible, trustworthy people? There's only one way."

"You trust them with information," Marvin said.

"And that means action, not words or smiles. You've got to show you trust them by sharing all kinds of information—even sensitive information. Have you talked a lot about empowering people in your company?"

"We sure have—with no results to show for it!"

"The same thing happened to us," said Robert. "When we began talking about empowerment several years ago, that's all it was—just talk. Nobody really believed anything would happen. We all felt it was just the latest fad. One of my associates who has been around the company for many years said, 'Just wait—this too shall pass.'"

"Sandy kept going around saying things like, 'You gotta believe that the magic happens where the work force is.' But we didn't know if she and the other managers really meant it. It wasn't until she began to share information with everyone that we really started to believe. The sharing of what had once been confidential information about performance, profits, true market share, and such, made us realize that this was a safe place for us to think and use our real talents and knowledge."

Marvin looked again at the card Robert had given him. "I'm beginning to see the real reason behind this first key. Information sharing to me was always purely functional—you know, linked to people's functions in the organization. So when you gave me this card, one of the reasons I resisted was not understanding why people needed all this information to do their jobs. Now I realize they need this information to become responsible and to feel trusted!"

"That's it!" exclaimed Robert.

"But what about goals?" sighed Marvin. "Throughout my career I've always understood that goal setting should be first. If information comes first, where do goals fit in?"

Robert smiled and said, "I was waiting for you to ask that, because everyone does. Goals are still very important.

"In most organizations goals are established at the top and then handed down. People feel no commitment to them because they haven't been involved in establishing them. I think you can sense how that wouldn't work in an empowered organization. To break down the traditional hierarchical belief that all the 'brains' are at the top of the organization, you have to start building trust first. Once information sharing takes place, and people have begun the journey together toward the Land of Empowerment, then goal setting takes on real meaning."

"So basically, you're telling me to wait and see," Marvin said.

"That's right," Robert agreed. "Remember, information sharing is only the first step on the journey. I'd like to tell you more, but I've got to get back to an urgent project right now. Why don't you talk to some other associates about additional keys to empowering people? Janet Wo over in production is someone I've worked with a lot. I happen to know that Janet has a meeting this afternoon, but let me call her and see if she'll meet with you tomorrow morning."

Robert set up a meeting for 8 A.M. the next day. Marvin left the building, his mind racing with thoughts about the sharing of information. When he reached the parking lot he sat in his car for a while, summarizing in his notebook what he had learned:

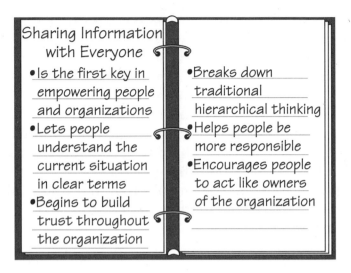

Sharing Information
with Everyone
- Is the first key in empowering people and organizations
- Lets people understand the current situation in clear terms
- Begins to build trust throughout the organization
- Breaks down traditional hierarchical thinking
- Helps people be more responsible
- Encourages people to act like owners of the organization

As he drove home, Marvin thought about how the new things he had learned clashed with his former beliefs and attitudes. I wonder what the other keys are, he thought. And will they be as big a surprise as the first one was?

T he next morning Marvin was back bright and early. As he entered the production area, a woman approached him and introduced herself as Janet Wo.

"I understand you've been hanging out with some of my colleagues—Sandy Fitzwilliam and Robert Borders," said Janet. "This stuff about empowering people can be pretty confusing at first. Remembering how it was for me, I imagine your head is spinning."

"Well, you're right," said Marvin. "I was surprised to learn how sharing information works to establish trust and help people improve their work processes. But I know that information alone can't be enough. What comes next?"

"To answer that question, let me ask you to consider things from the viewpoint of management. In order for people to be empowered, do you think they need more structure or less?"

"Why, less structure, of course. To empower people, you want to free them up, not restrict them with rules."

"Okay," Janet replied in a noncommittal way. "Now, think about where people are when you embark on the journey to the Land of Empowerment. They've heard about empowerment. Most of them probably want to be empowered. But what's their total experience of what it means to be empowered?"

"Zero."

"That's right."

"I see," Marvin mused. "They'd be lost. Maybe they would need structure after all."

"They would, but it's a different kind of structure," said Janet. With that, she handed Marvin another laminated card:

> *The second key*
> *is to*
> *create autonomy*
> *through boundaries.*

"People have to learn new ways of thinking and working together," Janet went on. "To use an analogy, in the old horse-and-buggy days people used to throw the reins over the horse's neck, and the horse would take them home. That worked because the horse knew the way, but people didn't do that when they were starting out on a new journey."

"What you're saying is that with a lack of guidelines, people revert back to their old unempowered habits—they head back home to the familiar," Marvin ventured.

Janet nodded. "Yes. Boundaries have the capacity to channel energy in a certain direction. It's like a river—if you were to take away the banks, the river wouldn't be a river anymore. Its momentum and direction would be gone."

"I guess a river without banks would be a very big puddle," said Marvin, laughing. "I see what you mean. You want people's energy to have direction and impact."

"Also, consider the security there is in having boundaries," added Janet. "How would you like to play tennis with just the net—there would be no lines to define a court. You wouldn't know how to keep score, what good performance was, or how to improve your game."

Marvin thought for a few seconds and then said, "I asked Robert where goal setting fits in and he essentially told me to be patient. Aren't goals an important part of this boundary process?"

"Absolutely," said Janet. "But there are other kinds of boundaries besides goal setting." Janet walked over to a file cabinet and rummaged through a drawer until she found what she wanted. "Here's a list of the critical areas where we started to create new boundaries," she said.

Boundary Areas
That Create Autonomy

1. **Purpose**—What business are you in?

2. **Values**—What are your operational guidelines?

3. **Image**—What is your picture of the future?

4. **Goals**—What, when, where, and how do you do what you do?

5. **Roles**—Who does what?

6. **Organizational Structure and Systems**—How do you support what you want to do?

"That looks like a lot of structure and boundaries to create," said Marvin.

"It is," answered Janet, "but it need not all be done at the same time. In fact, it can't. It must be done as you need it. In our company it began with top management drafting a compelling vision of our company as an empowered organization."

"A compelling vision," echoed Marvin.

"Yes," said Janet. "A compelling vision involves the first three boundary areas on our list. It emotionally and intellectually captivates the members of your organization and crystallizes their needs, desires, values, and beliefs. The way to create a compelling vision is to articulate a picture of the future, an *image*, which clarifies the *purpose* of your organization—what business you are in—and illuminates the guiding *values*."

"Give me an example," said Marvin.

"Sure. Steve Jobs of Apple Computer envisioned everyone using a personal computer. The *purpose* of the company was to build and make available affordable information systems—computers. The underlying *value* was to create access to an easy-to-use computer for everyone, not for just a few. The *image* of the end result was a personal computer on every desk and in every household. As his vision became clear, the means to achieve it also became clear, so Jobs developed a method to mass-produce high-quality personal computers. A compelling vision creates the big picture for your company."

"Did everyone get involved in clarifying your vision?"

"They sure did," smiled Janet. "Each person in every department translated the vision into roles and goals that had meaning for them personally. We call that defining the little picture."

"I always think in analogies," Janet continued. "In this case, I think of a jigsaw puzzle. The organizational vision is the big picture you end up with when you complete the puzzle. The specific role each person has to play in achieving the vision is like one individual puzzle piece. Each piece of the puzzle has a small picture on it that contributes to the big picture. In terms of our organization, each role has its own little picture."

"When you put it that way, each person's little picture is pretty important," Marvin said.

"Absolutely. It's a translation of the big picture into the specific actions that an associate performs. Those actions are directed toward goal accomplishment. For associates to be effective, they must see both the big picture *and* their role in achieving that picture."

"Most organizations do goal setting," said Marvin. "How is your process different in the context of empowerment?"

"Our goal-setting process focuses energy. Without clear goals people can waste energy."

"Waste energy?" wondered Marvin.

"Yes," said Janet. "Have you ever had your employees list ten things they think you hold them accountable for?"

"Why would I do that?" replied Marvin. "We tell them what's expected of them, and they all get annual performance reviews."

"You may have just diagnosed one of your biggest problems," said Janet. "Tell me, when people leave their performance review sessions with you, do they feel validated or surprised?"

Marvin reflected on the last three reviews he'd completed. "Come to think of it, they act surprised. Two of my last three reviews involved disagreements. The people said they didn't know they were responsible for certain areas."

"Sounds like you'd find the *Top Ten Planner* helpful. Since there is often a difference between what people think they're supposed to be doing on a day-to-day basis and what their manager thinks they should be doing, I recommend that each of them make a list and compare the priority of things on the two lists. Let me give you an example of how this *Top Ten Planner* works.

"A couple who are friends of mine own a convenience store. They were constantly in a quandary as to why things they thought were important weren't getting done around the store. So they asked their assistant to list the ten things she thought she was accountable for. This is the list the assistant produced." Janet handed Marvin a slip of paper:

1. Shrink (inventory loss)

2. Cash over or short on the register

3. Stock shelves

4. Clean rest rooms

5. Test gas tanks for water

6. Fresh coffee at all times

7. Clean parking lot

8. Organize back room

9. Rotate stock

10. Ordering

"My friends, the owners, made a list of the ten things they held the assistant accountable for. It looked like this." She gave him another slip of paper:

1. Sales volume

2. Profit

3. Customer perception

4. Quality of service

5. Cash management

6. Overall store appearance

7. Just-in-time inventory

8. Training employees

9. Protecting assets (maintenance)

10. Merchandise display

"When they compared lists, the problem became obvious. And as they told me about it they said, 'The fault turned out to be ours as managers. We tell people we'll hold them accountable for end results—such as sales, service, and so on. But the things we talk to them about day-in and day-out—the things that stick in their minds—are routine tasks. We were sending mixed messages. The *Top Ten Planner* really helped us to see what we were doing and to appreciate the pain we were causing our assistant as a result.

"'We'd been telling her things like:

- Shrink is too high.

- Why is the second shift twelve dollars short?

- There are holes in the shelf stock.

- The bathroom is a mess.

- Have you tested the gas tanks for water yet?

- You're out of coffee.

- Who had a party in the parking lot?

- Looks like you cleaned the stockroom with a hand grenade!

- Put the new product in the back.

- Your order is late.'

"People will never be empowered if they're not sure what their job is. Is it maintenance tasks, or is it end results? In this case, the fact that the assistant didn't make the connection between tasks and goals was the owners' fault."

"The owners daily feedback to the assistant fed the wrong goals. They should have been saying things like:

- Let me help you figure out why sales are down.

- What can we do to increase sagging profits?

- Let's find out what our customers think about no coffee and dirty rest rooms.

- Our gas customers have an impact on the impulse buying that is an important part of this business. Let's make sure they never get water in their gas tanks.

- If our cash is continually over or short, customers are probably being ripped off.

- First impressions are important. What do you think of the parking lot this morning?

- If the stock room isn't organized, we may have to tell a customer we're out of stock simply because we can't find a product.

- What employee training have you conducted this week?

- What is your schedule for rotating the displays so customers see different products?"

"The difference is what we talk to people about and the way we talk to them," said Marvin. "It's more like being a partner than being told what to do. I think that if I were the assistant and heard these kinds of messages consistently, I'd have more of a business perspective and feel more ownership."

"We've learned a lot from that story in our company," said Janet. "We've found that without clear goals that are consistently checked, people can't perform well or be empowered. In fact, highly skilled, creative people will waste a lot of time on less important activities, all the while believing they are doing what is expected of them. In the convenience store example, that might have meant that customers were waiting while someone swept the parking lot."

"I think I've got it," said Marvin. "The connection between boundaries and autonomy is getting clearer. I've tried to summarize it on paper in a way that makes sense to me." Marvin showed Janet his notebook:

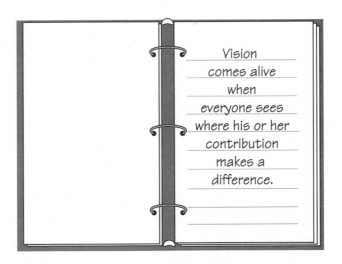

Vision
comes alive
when
everyone sees
where his or her
contribution
makes a
difference.

Janet chuckled and said, "Robert told me to watch out for you."

"What do you mean?"

"He said that while you might be resistant at first, once you grasp an idea, it doesn't take you long to run with it."

"Yeah, I guess so. I'm glad to find out where goal setting fits in, but tell me a little more about values," said Marvin.

"Values are a key element of a compelling vision," said Janet. "As we began our journey toward the Land of Empowerment, we found we had to clarify our fundamental beliefs and then translate them into commonly agreed-upon values. The former supports the vision, the latter makes it a reality. You see, organizations don't really have values until the associates who work there verify the statements of belief as the way to operate. So Sandy involved us in a collaborative process of validating our values."

"How did she do that?"

"First she gave us a talk on values. Everybody around here remembers that talk like it was yesterday. People refer to it as her 'I Have a Dream' speech."

"What did she say?"

"*What* she said was pretty important, but the *way* she said it was what really got our attention. It was like she was consulting with us. You can't listen to her long without hearing her commitment to certain values. She spelled these out for us, but in such a way that it was obvious that they would work and that they were our values, too."

"She made us feel important—just like she did when she gave us all that privileged information. Except this time it wasn't, 'I can't believe she's telling us this!' It was, 'I can't believe she's asking us!'"

"You mean you felt really involved," Marvin said with a smile.

"Yes. When somebody trusts you like that and asks for your involvement in clarifying values, you say to yourself, 'Why would I work anywhere else?' That speech was only the beginning, though. It was the validation process that followed that eventually got us all aligned with the same values."

"You mean you had an actual method of finding agreement on values?" Marvin asked.

"Everyone supported the values that Sandy articulated. The agreement was more about the rules surrounding those values," answered Janet. "In our work groups we were given a series of directions for creating departmental dialogues. We discussed the values and the ways they would be acted out in our work."

"How did the meetings go?"

"There were some real surprises at first."

"How so?"

"We didn't know that we had been operating under differing assumptions until we were involved in the process. As we tried to agree on ways we would operate and treat each other, we kept getting blocked. Once we started discussing the values and listening to each other, as the directions told us to do, our eyes were opened. Defining what was meant by certain key value words became the most important part of the exercise.

"Again and again," continued Janet, "I heard people say, 'I never dreamed you looked at it that way!' One of the guys in my unit said that when we started out we were like a bunch of iron filings, all spread out and pointing in different directions. The validating process was like a magnet passing over us, leaving us all aligned in unison."

"But that must have taken a lot of work time," Marvin said.

"As managers, we thought so, too," Janet replied. "We were asking, 'Why are we doing all this stuff, when we need to be filling orders and making money?' But you know what? That process eventually saved us time! It was amazing!"

"How do you mean?"

"Ever since the values process, decision making has been much faster and easier. We have a shared set of values to guide us."

"I've just made another discovery about my own organization," Marvin said. "We've been trying to get one simple statement across to everybody: 'If you see a problem, fix it.' Now I know why it's been so hard getting people to live by that statement."

"Oh?"

"The way we went about it was doubly wrong. First, people didn't choose the rule—it was imposed upon them. Second, we had no process for listening to each other and reaching agreement, like your process for validating values. For all I know, there are as many interpretations of what that statement means as there are people in the company!"

"Without agreement on a rule, you can't focus energy on your purpose. Values serve as the driving force for purpose. All parts of your compelling vision have to be integrated," said Janet.

"Tell me how structure and systems fit in," asked Marvin.

"Your vision tells you the right things to do, while your structure and systems, together with defined roles and goals, ensure that things are done right. Let me give you an example," said Janet. "We wanted to coordinate our production activities with our sales districts, so we suggested to the sales teams that we needed to improve planning. They were sympathetic, but when it came right down to it they wouldn't make the necessary changes in implementing the planning. Want to know why?"

"Sure."

"Their bonus was calculated on a formula that counted 'planning time' as 'nonproductive.' Planning time reduced their bonus! Once we changed the reward structure, the problem went away."

"So, organizational structures and systems that are already in place may hinder the process of empowering people to improve?"

"Right," said Janet. "But remember, these policies were created to support a control-oriented organization, not an empowered one."

Marvin thought about that. Then he said, "There are policies in my company that would inhibit people from being empowered. One is the requirement of a sign-off for purchases over certain amounts. Another is the demand for formal proposals on any changes that affect more than one department. The list goes on and on."

"Fortunately," assured Janet, "you can deal with each one as you go along. We found that the trust created by shared information made people feel free to express themselves about what was getting in the way of being empowered."

"Right there," said Marvin, "might be another reason for using the first key—sharing information—to start the process. It creates the basis of trust for the other steps. How did people express themselves, once they felt free to do so?"

"The question we heard most often was, 'Why do we do things this way?' Sandy encouraged it. Before long, everyone seemed to be examining every rule and policy and system to make sure it contributed to creating an empowered organization. In many cases the existing rules did contribute to empowering people. But a lot of other things went out the window. The whole organization took on a leaner, more streamlined feel. There were other important questions like, What is my new role? What do I get to decide? How will I be held accountable? What are the new rules? How do I get some training on my new role?"

"All those questions must make for lots of uncertainty," said Marvin.

"Actually, questions are the *result* of uncertainty," Janet smiled. "Change is always fraught with uncertainty. But in an information-sharing environment, where people operate with trust, uncertainty is something you can handle by communicating, getting agreement, and taking action. Such questions are a way of asking for clarification about the new boundaries."

"You know," said Marvin, "I get a feeling you people here are in it for the long haul."

"Yes, it's a journey. We don't have to do it all at once! I notice you've been writing lots of notes in your book. May I see what you've written?"

"Sure," replied Marvin. He showed Janet his notebook:

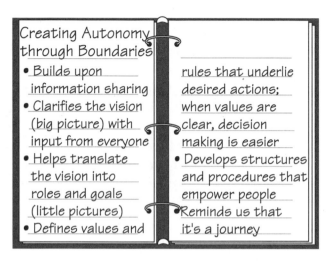

Creating Autonomy through Boundaries

- Builds upon information sharing
- Clarifies the vision (big picture) with input from everyone
- Helps translate the vision into roles and goals (little pictures)
- Defines values and

rules that underlie desired actions; when values are clear, decision making is easier
- Develops structures and procedures that empower people
- Reminds us that it's a journey

"Hey, that's great. You've got it," said Janet.

"Something is still missing," said Marvin. "Information sharing, clarifying boundaries—what else?"

"To learn about the third key for the journey to the Land of Empowerment I suggest that you talk to Billy Abrams over in Customer Service.

"Good luck to you on your journey, Marvin," Janet said. "I'd like to leave you with something Sandy said that has always appealed to me: 'Empowerment isn't magic—just some simple ideas and a lot of smart work.'"

As Marvin headed over to meet Billy Abrams, he was thinking, simple ideas and a lot of smart work. That's what I want for my company.

Marvin saw Billy Abrams hurrying toward him as he entered the Customer Service work area. Right away he sensed Billy was a high-energy person like himself—not much on talk and a pragmatist when it came to ideas.

As Billy led Marvin through the work area, Marvin said, "I sense you're a busy man, and I want to thank you for taking the time to meet with me. As you may know, I'm here to learn the third key to empowerment."

"No problem," said Billy, as if dismissing his last statement. "Tell me, did your company recently go through downsizing?"

"Yes, we did," answered Marvin. "It's tough being responsible for eliminating jobs."

"I know what you mean. The same thing happened in this company."

"But in retrospect, it was absolutely necessary," Marvin quickly added, "to survive and thrive as an organization. In order to be responsive to customers, we needed a company with as few management layers as possible."

Billy and Marvin strolled through groups of industrious people. A couple of associates were talking excitedly together in front of a computer screen. They looked up, smiled enthusiastically, and then went back to their task, as Billy and Marvin walked by.

"Let me ask you something," Billy said. "When you finish flattening an organization by eliminating jobs, outsourcing services, and cutting out middle layers of management, what kind of a situation are you left with?"

"Well . . . ," Marvin said slowly. He started counting on the fingers of one hand. "You've got upper management closer to where the action is. You've got supervisors with a wider span of control. And you've got resentful people who have been trained to carry out decisions made by others with 'privileged information' who they no longer trust."

"Exactly," said Billy. "All you're describing is a smaller bureaucracy with fewer layers and more negative attitudes. Decision making is still moving up the hierarchy. If we want an empowered organization, all that has to change. So the burning question becomes: What's going to take the place of the old hierarchy in terms of decision making?"

Marvin began, "It seems like it would be everyone's responsibility now. But you can't just have an organization of autonomous people acting in isolation from each other. Maybe we need to depend on people working together in teams. People in teams can build off each other's specialized skills and knowledge. Yes, I'd vote for teams."

Billy nodded. They had been standing in the midst of a bustling stream of people. Billy led the way over to a couple of chairs at a table on the edge of the work area. Then he handed Marvin a laminated card:

> ### The third key
> ### is to
> ### replace the hierarchy
> ### with self-directed teams.

"Replace is a harsh word. I don't know how you can do that!" exclaimed Marvin.

"Before the change, we'd had participative management and work teams. But they had always been in the context of the traditional hierarchy—mostly one-way communication, with decisions being handed down the line from the top. At best, the teams made recommendations; the managers made the decisions."

"But we realized we were faced with new competition. In our leaner organization we had to stay close to the customer and yet still maintain internal controls that would protect our financial interests. The old hierarchy was too slow and cumbersome to accomplish that. And, as you implied, a team of empowered people is far more powerful than a disconnected set of individuals. So the solution was to get teams to do much of what the management hierarchy had done in the past. Our people had to learn to work in self-directed teams and to make and implement their decisions. Even at the lowest level, people began to grapple with the kinds of responsibilities that had always been left to managers."

"What's a self-directed team?" Marvin asked.

"It's a unique kind of team. It consists of a group of employees with responsibility for an entire process or product. They plan, perform, and manage the work from start to finish."

"Does the team have a manager?"

"There may be a manager on a team," explained Billy. "But, if it's a high-performing team, you'd never be able to pick that person out. Everyone shares equally in the responsibilities. They might rotate team leadership, but the group would decide how."

"That must have been quite a change!" exclaimed Marvin.

"It happened right here," said Billy as he looked around. "The people you see in this department have become part of high-performing, self-directed teams."

"You say that very proudly," Marvin said.

"The mission of our department is an important one," Billy said. "We're really the sensing arm of the organization and the problem-solving arm for the customer. We're concerned with anything that goes wrong in the company's effort to serve customers. When an error occurs, we immediately gather all the information about it. Then we feed that information to our production and billing operations so that they understand what's been done wrong and can correct it for the future."

"Sounds like a big responsibility," said Marvin.

"It is," agreed Billy. "On the other hand, it's not too large when viewed as a team effort. No one person has to do it alone. In fact, we who are on customer service teams can't even do it by ourselves. It's the whole organization's responsibility to provide good customer service. Our teams just lead the effort. The point you need to realize is that as teams we are constantly functioning the way only managers did in the past—assessing information from all over the company, analyzing that information, deciding what to do about it, and relaying our decisions to others."

"Hmm," said Marvin. "I can see that people aren't sitting around waiting to be told what to do next. I've been watching your associates as we've been talking. They obviously count on each other, but everybody acts like a manager. In a hierarchical operation, people just do their assigned jobs; they don't go out of their way to help someone else. But here, everyone who comes by looks at me and smiles. I can sense their high energy and enthusiasm. They act committed—like it's their company."

"Right, but you've got to realize that it hasn't always been that way," said Billy, smiling. "In the beginning, my associates and I were—well, let's just say we were not immediately committed to this team idea. Many of us thought the idea of being a self-directed team sounded good, but we had no experience or understanding of how it would work."

"That's where the people are in my company," Marvin said. "I have all these wonderful ideas from the past two days to bring to them about empowerment and building self-directed teams, but they probably haven't a clue about how to begin to operate in this new way."

Marvin paused and then said, "It's like wanting something to function freely by itself, but in order for it to do that you have to give it a push."

"That's a very good way of talking about the paradox you experience in the beginning, before people are empowered."

"You can't just stand around hoping they'll take over. You have to start by giving them what they need at the place where they are. In our case, the managers had to begin with a rather directive style of leadership."

"I've been getting that message," said Marvin. "Autonomy begins with the need for boundaries and direction."

"Right," said Billy. "Guidelines and structure are essential in the beginning of the empowerment journey. People think directive behavior is telling people *how* to do their jobs, but our managers put the emphasis on telling us how to *manage* our jobs.

"It was exciting to suddenly be charged with using all the job knowledge we'd accumulated as a group. Almost everyone had ideas about how we could improve our service and responsiveness to our customers. But we didn't know how to make decisions as a team. We lacked team skills—skills for solving problems, managing meetings, managing the team, and handling conflict."

"So your managers focused their directive leadership not on telling you what to do but on developing the skills that were going to enable you to function on your own as a team."

"Right."

Marvin had been summarizing in his notebook again. He showed Billy what he had written:

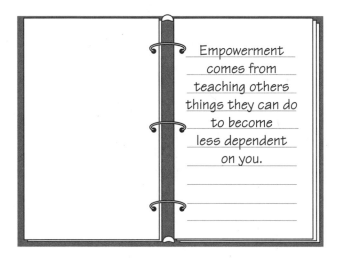

Empowerment
comes from
teaching others
things they can do
to become
less dependent
on you.

"That beautifully captures the idea for the starting point in training teams," responded Billy. "It was a lesson managers throughout our company had to learn the hard way.

"In the beginning, they thought the idea was to leave self-directed teams alone. So they abdicated their roles as coaches and then wondered why teams floundered. Everyone on our team was excited at first. But that lasted only for about a week. Then came denial—nobody wanted to admit we were totally confused. We did not want to recognize the widespread dissatisfaction."

"So what happened?" asked Marvin. "Obviously things got straightened out."

"What happened was that Sandy recognized the state of chaos we were in. She called us all together to help diagnose the trouble. She took the blame for the confusion and never pointed a finger at anyone else. That showed us that management was on our side.

"In the meeting we realized that we wanted to be empowered but that we lacked many of the necessary skills. Together we concluded that we needed training in how to become a self-directed team. We needed strong leadership to guide and direct us. And we needed careful monitoring of our progress."

"In effect, you were asking managers to direct you," said Marvin. "So your managers began with a strong directive style. But I assume that to become empowered, sooner or later they had to stop using that style with you. Remember, you said when you become a high-performing team, you can't tell who's the leader. How did the team get away from the need for the directive leadership?"

"Slowly. Gradually. Almost imperceptibly at first," responded Billy. "Then faster. We began to hear stories of people and teams acting in empowered ways. Teams began to do things that only managers had done in the past, and do them better. Our managers began to act like facilitators and coaches."

"Some of them started to be masters at choosing just the right moment to do what we call 'standing there.'"

"What's that?"

"It's actually a critical skill of managing to empower. You have to know when to follow the rule:

Don't just
do something—
stand there.

"You mean knowing when *not* to step in so that somebody else can act?" asked Marvin.

"Yes. The managers became adept at gradually transferring more and more responsibilities to the teams. Their fears dissipated as they found that there was still plenty for them to do—things like more involvement in strategic planning, working more with customers, looking at new equipment and procedures, researching and delivering the kind of training people will need in the future, as well as special company projects that have been on the back burner."

"There's a delicate balance to this matter of transferring," Marvin ventured.

"It's a dance," said Billy. "Like dancing, though, once you get the hang of it, you trust your intuition. In empowering people and teams, you learn new ways of assessing people. The best part is watching employees become associates. It's a lot of fun to 'lead' them occasionally to just a little bit more responsibility than they think they can handle. Then when it turns out you were right and they do handle it, it's great to see the pride in their faces!"

Marvin paused, thought for a moment, and said, "You know, this team thing—correction, this empowered-team thing—can really be powerful. It's like a basketball team or a volleyball team that plays really well together. The team members' skills are transferable but also unique. They are given a chance to utilize their abilities and to continue to grow and develop. As individuals, they have the chance to become all that they can be and, at the same time, they're helping the organization become all that it can possibly be."

"It sounds like you've got it," said Billy.

"Yeah, maybe," said Marvin, "but to make sure, why don't you take a look at this?" Marvin handed his notebook over to Billy:

Replace the
Hierarchy with
Self-Directed Teams
- Empowered teams can do more than empowered individuals
- People don't start out knowing how to work in self-directed teams
- Dissatisfaction is a natural step in the process
- Everyone has to be trained in team skills
- Commitment and support have to come from the top
- Teams with information and skills can replace the old hierarchy

"You're right on the money," said Billy with a smile.

"You're a good teacher," insisted Marvin.

After Marvin thanked Billy, he headed home. As he drove, Marvin could not stop thinking about what he had learned. One burning question that he wished he could answer kept coming to the surface. Finally, it got to him. He picked up the car phone and dialed Sandy Fitzwilliam's number.

"I wondered when I would hear from you again," she said.

"May I come by to talk with you right now?" Marvin asked.

"Of course. I'll be waiting."

As Marvin walked into Sandy's office, he found her in a familiar pose, staring out the window. As she turned to greet him, he jumped right into his question, "So far, I've learned three keys to empowerment. They sound good, but do they work? Do they make a difference in performance or results?"

She responded, "Slow down a minute, and tell me what you've learned."

"Okay. I've learned that there are three keys to empowerment that are part of a process for releasing the potential that is within people."

Marvin showed her his summary notes:

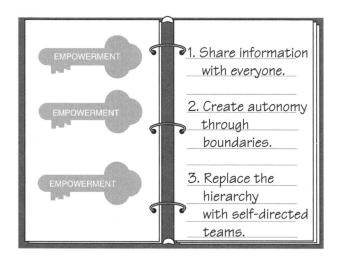

After Sandy read his notes, Marvin started talking excitedly again, continually referring to his cards and notes. For twenty minutes he talked without letting her say a word. She sat back in her chair and listened intently.

When Marvin finished, he was a bit out of breath. He looked at the Empowering Manager and waited for her to say something. Finally she spoke. "It's evident to me that you understand the steps for creating an empowered organization. You get an *A* for your solid grasp of the main ideas."

"But can these three keys really lead to empowerment?" Marvin asked. He had always been a bottom-line manager. "Isn't there more? Do they really improve performance and employee satisfaction?"

"Yes, yes, and yes," she replied with a smile. "Let me point out a few things regarding performance. This plant has far exceeded even my expectations as we moved to empowerment. Now don't misunderstand; we were the leading plant in our company even before empowerment, but we felt we could do better. And were we ever right!"

"Since we began the empowerment process," she continued, "our quality of production has exceeded 99.99 percent, while our costs have been cut 10 to 15 percent every year.

"On top of that, our people come to work excited every day; they find the increased responsibility very rewarding. And, they continue to come up with new ways to get work done faster, at lower cost, and with higher quality. Our business has been booming, and our customers love us."

"I'm impressed," said Marvin. "Tell me more about the performance and satisfaction that results from applying each of the three keys to empowerment."

"Once again I think you'd be better off talking to my colleagues," Sandy insisted. She picked up the phone and called Elizabeth Meadows in Shipping and found that Marvin could see her the next morning.

"Elizabeth has some great ideas," she said. "She's right there on the front line, and I think you'll find that she's a results-oriented manager who can give you some more insights, particularly about the impact of sharing information and creating boundaries."

71

"That would be helpful," said Marvin. "Do you have any final thoughts before I head off?"

"Two," Sandy replied. "First of all, as you may already have found, the three keys to empowerment are simple and easy to understand, but they are difficult to put into everyday action. And, second, the three keys need to be viewed as operating in dynamic interaction with each other. While information sharing is the critical first step, empowering people takes all three keys, with a constant shifting in emphasis as needed."

Marvin nodded, thinking, *all three in dynamic interaction.* Then he replied, "Thanks, that helps. I'm looking forward to meeting with Elizabeth Meadows."

Marvin arrived early the next morning, hoping that Elizabeth could show him that empowerment worked.

As he reached the Shipping area, Marvin was greeted by a tall, middle-aged woman. "Hi. I'm Elizabeth Meadows, and this is the area my associates and I own."

"What do you mean, you own it?" Marvin asked.

"I mean," smiled Elizabeth, "we have all the information we need to make any important decision that has to be made to serve the customer, ensure quality, and make a profit for our company."

"Maybe that explains what happened when I was walking down here to meet you this morning," Marvin said. "I overheard one of the Shipping people telling someone on the phone that the missing items would be replaced at no cost and sent overnight to arrive tomorrow. Frankly, I was amazed. People in Shipping don't usually have the authority to make that kind of decision."

Elizabeth, who had been peering over her half-glasses as she listened, said, "Right. But people in Shipping who have information can make that kind of decision and know that it won't hurt the company. In fact, with information they would know just what dividends such excellent customer service will pay in the future. They can weigh the cost against the benefit of replacing the item at no cost."

"How can they know that?" asked Marvin.

Elizabeth gestured to indicate the area around them. "Information!" she said with a smile.

For the first time, Marvin really took in the graphs and charts that were everywhere on the walls, the computer screens filled with figures, and the people working quickly and with little or no supervision.

"It's impressive all right," Marvin said hesitantly. "But I'm still skeptical about whether information sharing really works. As a matter of fact, that's why I came back to talk to Sandy Fitzwilliam. I need to know that the three keys to empowerment really work. I want results."

Elizabeth looked over her glasses into Marvin's eyes. Then she asked, "Do you ever write a check to pay for groceries at the supermarket? The cashier verifies your ID and writes the number on the check, right? Then what happens?"

"I usually wait around while the cashier calls the manager or assistant manager to come over and approve the check," answered Marvin. "The manager's talking to someone two aisles over as he or she is initialing the check. Now that I think about it, it doesn't seem right—especially since the 'wake-up call' you have given me."

"Why isn't it right?" asked Elizabeth.

"It sends a message that the store doesn't trust the cashiers and that the only employees there who have brains are the managers. The rest of the people might as well leave their brains at home because maybe they'll need them after work."

"Right," said Elizabeth. "In that process, what do you suppose happens to the cashier's self-esteem?"

"It's eroded."

"Right again. Now, what do you think would happen if the cashiers were given all the detailed information about the impact that bad checks have on the business, and then were given check approval power?"

"Fewer bounced checks," Marvin responded.

"Right! That's what all the research says about places where it's been done. Further, the people have higher self-esteem and can provide more attentive customer service. When you give people information and a chance to act like owners, they'll usually come through," Elizabeth explained.

"Give me another example," Marvin requested.

"Sure," said Elizabeth. "A friend of mine owns a restaurant. I was telling her about the power of sharing information with her people. She just wasn't buying it. She didn't think certain information was any of her people's business. To help her move from her 'stuck' position, I had her call together all the folks who work at her restaurant one night at closing time—the hostess, waiters, dish washers, chef, everyone—and had her sit them down at tables in small groups and answer the following question: 'Of every sales dollar that comes into this restaurant, how many cents do you think go to the bottom line as profit that can be returned to me as an owner or reinvested in the business?'"

"What did they say?" Marvin asked.

"The lowest guess was 45 cents and the highest was 75 cents. When my friend told them the correct answer was 8 cents, they were shocked. They thought the restaurant was a money machine. Imagine what that misconception did to their attitude toward things like breakage and food wastage."

"They wouldn't care," said Marvin.

"That's for sure," replied Elizabeth. "What really convinced my friend I was right about the power of sharing information was the remark the head chef made: 'You mean if I burn a six-dollar steak that we charge the customer fifteen dollars for, we have to sell at least five steaks to recover the six-dollar loss?' He had it figured out, and so did everyone else."

"Interesting," mused Marvin. "So they started thinking in business terms. Did it make any difference?"

"Last year my friend declared, 'None of you will get a raise unless you can read our balance sheet and explain what it means.' And for the first time the restaurant showed over a 10 percent profit. When my friend shared 25 percent of that new profit with her staff, they were thrilled and started talking about additional ways they could cut costs and increase profits in the future."

"So you have to *show* people that you trust them by sharing information," commented Marvin.

Elizabeth made another sweeping gesture toward the department and said, "As I said before, this place belongs to us. We own it! Now you can understand what our banner means," she said, pointing to a banner on the wall:

> Give people the information to act;
> then look for magic to happen!

"Fascinating," said Marvin. "How has this worked for you?"

"I've learned that once you share information and trust starts to develop, you can begin to establish high standards," said Elizabeth. "You can talk about closing the gaps between what's happening today in terms of cost, profits, and so on, and what's possible tomorrow, and it makes sense to everyone."

"Sounds like the TQM idea of continuous improvement," Marvin interjected.

"It is," replied Elizabeth. "Continuous improvement only makes sense when people have information and are trusted to use their skills and abilities. That brings me to another important learning. See that?" Elizabeth pointed to a sign:

**Every
"misteak"
is an opportunity
to increase
competence.**

"Sandy had these signs posted around the company when we began our journey. Again, everyone thought she was a few bricks short of a full load. The way you're looking at me, I'd say you think so, too."

"It bothers me," Marvin said. "I'm a stickler for details, so I want to correct the spelling on your sign. More importantly, I don't want mistakes made in our organization. What does making mistakes have to do with improving performance?"

"Let me ask you something," said Elizabeth. "When a mistake is made in your organization, what's the first question asked, 'What can we learn?' or 'Who is to blame?'"

Marvin answered, "Most times it's, 'Who is to blame?'"

"Sure," agreed Elizabeth. "Now, what is continuous improvement but innovation? And blaming kills the spirit of innovation. People can't innovate while they're busy protecting themselves. On the other hand, permission to take risks, make mistakes, and challenge the way things have been done in the past opens up people's ability to learn and use their talents. That's why Sandy wanted associates here to see mistakes as okay—to be lighthearted about them—to celebrate them, even."

"Interesting," Marvin said. "It reminds me of an article I read about encouraging innovation. I couldn't understand when it mentioned that one company shoots off a cannon every time there's a goof. Now I get it."

"Incidentally," Elizabeth grinned, "if you did go over and correct the spelling on the sign, you'd have some associates here frowning. Since everyone's gotten the message, *m-i-s-t-e-a-k* has become the official spelling of *mistake* in our company."

"You mean they're protective of their right to make errors?"

"In a way, I suppose they are. What do you think happens when people are encouraged to make mistakes? Do you think they act more responsibly, or less?"

Marvin thought about that. He realized he'd come up against a basic belief about people. "I used to think they would act less responsibly. Now I want to think they'd act more responsibly. What have you found?"

"They do. That's a significant outcome of empowerment. Shifting the definition of a mistake from something bad or wrong to an opportunity to learn encourages people to think and to monitor their own performance. In other words, it empowers them. And what we're learning, again and again, is that when people are empowered, they perform at a higher level. What we must do is hold people accountable for nothing but the best, while recognizing that people must make mistakes to continue to improve."

"I've just figured out something about this matter of 'misteaks,'" Marvin said with a smile.

"When people are blamed for mistakes, they become self-protective. In fact, they'll cover up mistakes in an effort to avoid blame. This limits the information that flows from the mistake, information everyone could learn from."

"That emphasizes the trust-building element of sharing information," said Elizabeth. "But there are far more practical advantages to the strategy. Want to hear another example?"

Marvin nodded. Elizabeth pointed to a chalkboard that had "FOUR HOURS" written on it in large letters in the shipping work area.

"Therein lies a tale of continuous improvement based on information," said Elizabeth. "About a year ago we began to look at our performance. We learned that when customers ordered something, it was taking us three to five days before it was shipped. Until we got that information, we never thought much about it. Now that we had it, we wondered, 'Why should it take so long?' We did some checking and learned that in our industry the typical shipping time for an order was about two days. We wanted to do better than twice the industry average! We began to determine how we could improve.

"Now keep in mind that had we not had the information available to examine, we would not even have been aware of the need for improvement. Also, if some manager had just challenged us to ship orders quicker, we wouldn't have had the commitment."

"I see how that works," said Marvin. "The fact that you found it out yourself got you on your own case. And you didn't just know you needed to be better. You decided how much better you needed to be."

"Right. Once we saw the information—especially about how our performance compared to other companies—we knew we had to do something. We made the decision ourselves to change things right here in this department." Marvin was noticing the pride Elizabeth took in telling him this story. It was as if he were hearing the owner of the company talk.

"Within one month of becoming aware of the problem," Elizabeth continued excitedly, "we had cut the shipping time down to the two-day industry average, but we didn't stop there. We knew we could do better. We wanted to see how far we could take it. We continued to track information on our performance. We began to change the way we responded to orders. Every order was now seen as an opportunity to please a customer. Everyone pulled together as a team. Within another month we had cut our shipping time down to less than a day. And now, a year later, our typical shipping time is four hours."

"Four hours! Down from three to five days to four hours—that's incredible!" Marvin exclaimed.

"Amazing results can come from simply giving people the information with which to work, plus the freedom to operate with that information."

Marvin began to get excited. "Okay, I get it now. People's full talents can't be used by the organization when they don't feel safe and when they don't have information. When they do feel safe, free to experiment, and apprised of all the information management has, they develop the same feelings as owners. Owners are the ones who feel responsible for everything working right in the company, because they have the information to see a more complete picture. Owners don't hold back—they give the success of the company their full attention. When people begin to feel like owners, they begin to act like owners. Now you've got yourself a smarter, more competent organization."

"Right," said Elizabeth, "but let me add one important point: In an empowered organization, position power means very little. Instead we rely on expertise and relationships and on people taking responsibility for their own actions."

"I like that," said Marvin. He had a sudden insight about all the great computer technology his company had at its disposal. Up to this point only he and his managers had been using it to share and access sensitive information. Last week a consultant had made a dynamic presentation to his management team that included a demonstration of a new software product called Groupware. Whereas most PC software programs were written for people working alone, Groupware was designed to make it easier for people to work together.

Marvin thought, wouldn't that make it possible for people throughout the organization to have easy access to almost any information they needed, at the stroke of a few keys? He made some notes in his notebook, then looked up at Elizabeth.

"But I still wonder," said Marvin thoughtfully, "Does everyone really want to meet this challenge. Don't some people just want to get by?"

"Sure," said Elizabeth. "We've found that a small percentage of people simply don't want the extra responsibility and accountability that comes with having more information. But the vast majority do. It's a matter of reactivating their natural desire."

"You think that people would rather be magnificent than ordinary, right?"

"Exactly," said Elizabeth. "It's just that their desire for magnificence is . . . well . . . dormant. For years in many organizations you were promoted by doing what you were told. 'Don't rock the boat, and you'll get ahead' became a way of life."

"As a result," agreed Marvin, "people need to relearn how to take initiative, be responsible and empowered. I'm certainly learning that. Tell me more about how creating autonomy through boundaries makes a difference."

"Of course," agreed Elizabeth. "Why don't we walk over to the cafeteria and get a cup of coffee?"

As they strolled along, Elizabeth began to explain how various kinds of structure take on a new meaning in an empowered organization.

"Once people have the information to understand their current situation, boundaries don't seem like constraints but rather guidelines for action. Take roles and goals for example. I'm sure Janet Wo talked to you about developing the big picture into little pictures."

"Yes, she did."

"That's important to us, because when it comes to defining roles and goals, our process is a two-way street. Management and informed people throughout the organization work together to develop the big picture, as well as their little pictures. When the vision is clear, everyone knows where their job and their work on individual tasks fits into a bigger perspective."

"Can you give me an example?" asked Marvin.

"Have you ever returned a new shirt because of a flaw and been told to take it and the receipt to Customer Service to get a voucher before you can come back and get a another one?"

"Yes," said Marvin. "What an inconvenience!"

"Last week," Elizabeth continued, "I went back to a store to exchange a blouse that had a button missing. They didn't have any others in my size. So the salesperson took out a box of buttons, found one that matched, and sewed the button on for me right there! I browsed around while I was waiting and ended up buying another blouse. That was a win for me and for the store, wasn't it? But think about why that worked so well. Not only was that woman a great salesperson but the training that she'd received provided boundaries that empowered her to help me."

"You mean, within certain guidelines the clerk had control over what to do," said Marvin. "The boundaries provided the playing field and the rules, and on that field the salesperson was free to play her own outstanding game."

Elizabeth smiled and nodded.

"That's certainly a new use of terms like *boundaries* and *structure* for me," continued Marvin. "In the past, people have become used to working within structure, but the structure's been there to inhibit action, limit thinking and risk taking, and correct mistakes by punishing those responsible."

"You're talking here about new rules and boundaries that encourage responsibility, ownership, and empowerment. How do you get people to make that shift? Won't there be all kinds of problems?"

"We certainly had our share of them," Elizabeth answered. "At first we tried eliminating most rules and structure and using slogans to guide us. But we found that didn't work. People cannot go from a controlled environment to complete freedom and autonomy overnight."

"That sounds like what Billy Abrams was telling me about creating self-directed work teams," said Marvin. "Managers have to start with strong, clear leadership and gradually move toward more supporting and delegating styles."

"Yes," Elizabeth affirmed. "There's a paradox here. You need rules and structure so that people are comfortable at first during the change over. But they are not the old rules and structures that dominated hierarchical life. These new boundaries must demonstrate the values that support your empowerment effort. I made a little desk card that many of us keep around as a reminder of this paradox:"

> *New boundaries help everyone learn to act with responsibility and autonomy.*

"Again," said Marvin, "I need an example."

"Good. This example demonstrates our value of 'recovery.' We had shipped some components to a customer, only to find that when the unit was assembled on site, it didn't fit into the space the architect had designed. Our people had met with the architect, visited the building site, and followed the specs to the letter, but somehow a mistake had been made. To correct it would cost us ten thousand dollars, which amounted to our entire profit for the job."

"That's a sticky one," Marvin said with a grimace. "What happened?"

"In the past," Elizabeth continued, "we would have put all our energy into identifying who was to blame—the architect, the customer, or someone in our company. But we have a guideline now that says, 'When a mistake is made, do whatever it takes to recover.' In our training we learned to ask, 'How can we recover so that the customer is happy and so that we get some good learning from this mistake?'"

"That's a great question!" Marvin exclaimed. "It's got integrity. How did you come up with it?"

"It came out of the values and dialogue process we all went through in the beginning. We have a group of rules like this that are basically values questions converted into rules of action."

"If that happened in my company," Marvin said, "Heads would have rolled after we satisfied the customer. So what happened?"

"We assured the customer that the problem would be fixed. Then while we worked with the contractor and architect to modify the space and the unit itself, we had people on the site charting all the changes, their costs, and the other processes of recovery. Later, a task force met to go over the records to see what we could learn from it."

"How did it all turn out?" Marvin asked. "I'm particularly interested in the financial impact on the company."

"We did more than keep a key customer. The way we handled it resulted in a major referral by that client to another string of companies with whom we've been doing business ever since. And we did get our ten thousand dollars worth of learning out of it. The story of that situation resulted in a renewal of commitment throughout the company of getting things right the first time. The situation assured us that we could 'walk our talk' by following our values-based guidelines instead of indulging in 'poor me' or blaming. It demonstrated the capacity of our structure to encourage people's problem-solving instincts, too.

"The key solution in this situation—modifying both the space and the unit—came from a person who had relatively little to do with the project, but her instincts were right on target. Also, the associates who contributed to the recovery project developed managerial thinking and expertise that has since proved invaluable."

That's a lot of payoff, thought Marvin. Then he said, "I see now that mistakes are opportunities to improve and use our talents, not times to find fault."

"You know," said Elizabeth, "it's great having the freedom to operate in this new structure. It's also great to find out that every day you can rise to the standards it implies for responsibility and accountability. There's a sign that hangs in what our team calls our 'powwow room' that reminds us of this:"

Empowerment
means you have
freedom
to act;
it also means
you are
accountable
for results.

"You've certainly added to my understanding about information and boundaries, Elizabeth," said Marvin. "And I've already taken up too much of your time today."

"It's been my pleasure," said Elizabeth warmly. "I was just about to suggest you talk to someone in Computer Services about self-directed teams. Luis Gomez over there has a story that will interest you. It's about the nervousness their team had about replacing the hierarchy. I'll walk you over.

"One more point," said Elizabeth as they walked to the Computer Services Department, "Nothing is static in the empowerment process. The boundaries we've been talking about will continue to evolve. The evolution will come from all over the organization. People will define goals for themselves and their peers. They'll suggest new roles and improvements. They'll use their teams far more effectively in some cases than you can expect at first. But I'm going to stop there. Telling you about teams is Luis's job."

M arvin was surprised to find how young yet seemingly well informed Luis Gomez was.

"So it's my job to show you more about how teams become the hierarchy," Luis told him when they met. "Actually, that's my favorite subject. Probably the fact that I'm team leader this quarter has something to do with it."

"Did top management give you some rules that govern your team's operation?" asked Marvin.

"We operate with very few rules from the top," Luis answered. "In fact, we have only four basic rules.

1. Keep customers first and foremost in our actions.

2. Look to the company's financial interests.

3. Be flexible in making quality decisions.

4. Keep others in the company informed."

"But," Marvin said, "I've just finished learning from Elizabeth that new rules and boundaries are essential for getting to empowerment."

"That's right, but they're essential mainly at the beginning of the process," Luis said. "We've come a long way on our journey to get where we are today. We started with a lot of external structure and rules. But now those rules come from within our team. Let me tell you how that happened."

"Good," said Marvin.

"More than two years ago when we began our journey," Luis said, "Sandy told us that her goal was not only to flatten the organizational pyramid but to turn it upside down for operating decisions."

"What did she mean by 'turn the pyramid upside down for operating decisions'?" asked Marvin.

"Suppose you have two phones on your desk, one red and one blue," said Luis. "The red phone is a direct line to the chairman of the board. The blue phone is a direct line to customers. Both phones start ringing at the same time. Which do you answer first?"

Marvin paused, then said, "Well, the red phone, of course!"

"Right. And that," said Luis, "is the problem with most organizations. The pyramid is inverted only when it's safe for you to answer the blue phone first."

"I happen to know that your company has gone through a downsizing like we did. But mere downsizing does little to change the fundamental way that work gets done in a corporation.

"Without taking some specific steps such as those you've been learning about here, it remains a typical, vertical organization. People continue to look up to their bosses instead of out to customers. Their loyalty is still to the functional fiefdoms in which they work rather than to the overall company and its goals."

"Exactly," Marvin replied emphatically, thinking of his own company.

Luis continued, "When people are empowered they don't look up the hierarchy for answers; they take responsibility to solve problems where they occur."

"How did your people respond to this new responsibility?" asked Marvin.

"At first, when people began to realize that they had more responsibility, many of them acted like they didn't want it. There were feelings left over from the old days when the attitude was 'That's not my job.' I remember hearing people say, 'If we're gonna be bosses, we should be getting more pay.' Handling this resistance to change was one of the functions of training that was critical to our efforts."

"What was the first thing you did to help change attitudes?" Marvin asked.

"Sandy kept preaching the belief that decisions had to be made at the lowest level of the organization."

"Don't you mean 'at the highest level of the organization'?"

"Good catch," laughed Luis. "For frontline managers to do that, people were going to need new skills and different ways to operate. In short, they had to learn to act in responsible, decision-making teams."

"How did people take that?"

"They were confused. On the one hand it sounded good, but they didn't know what it meant. Neither did the managers. Everyone became discouraged and confused about what to do next, because they had never done this before, either. It was a very frustrating period of time for everyone. It became clear you could not just announce empowerment and expect it to magically occur."

"That's what I've done," said Marvin, reflecting on the recent happenings at his company. "How did you pull out of this mess? Before I came to see Sandy and all of you, I was ready to throw in the towel and give up."

"We almost gave up ourselves," said Luis, "but then two things happened. First of all, Sandy didn't give up. She just persisted and kept talking to us as if we were all managers. A simple example is the *asking memo* she began to use."

"Asking memo?"

"You know how it goes in the typical unempowered organization: A memo comes down from on high saying we all need to start to save electricity or paper or some darn thing, and people stand around and look at each other, smile, and say, 'R-i-i-i-ght.' Then the manager comes out of his or her office and starts giving out orders about how it's to be done. Everybody feels like a naughty kid getting a lecture."

"That sounds like what I've seen, and done, all my life," sighed Marvin."

"That's a *telling memo,*" nodded Luis. "An *asking memo* is different. Take the case of the problem of saving resources. Sandy's memo would start out with the pertinent cost information, broken down to include the department's portion of the problem. The language of the memo would be short and sweet— no pep talk like, 'Let's all get behind this effort.' It would be written simply, as if the readers needed this information so they could make decisions about it. When people in our department received one of those early asking memos from Sandy, they looked at each other and then read the memo again. It was obvious that a departmental decision had to be made.

"It was just as obvious that no one was going to make it for us," Luis continued. "Pretty soon a dialogue would start. People would suggest things they could do. Then they'd decide what they *would* do."

"Early version of a team meeting," Marvin put in. "How about carrying out the decision?"

"A snap," replied Luis. "Since the group had dealt with the problem on its own, the group 'owned' the solution. You know the way it is whenever you have a joint agreement with somebody. You both feel willing to carry it out and also to tell the other person if he or she goofs."

Marvin nodded. "But I'm wondering about something. As you were developing these self-directed teams, what was the function of the managers?"

"That leads into the second thing that helped pull us through a period of high dissatisfaction and discouragement—training! Managers knew they should be behaving differently and so did their team members, but nobody had a clue what to do until Sandy required us all to go to training."

"Required you to go to training?" echoed Marvin.

"Yes," said Luis. "Sandy sees training not as an option but as a value. She made training a requirement for everybody. She said that once you're scheduled for training you cannot cancel it for any reason other than for a personal emergency. She said if we were ever tempted to pull someone from training we should call her, and she'd work the person's shift."

Luis excused himself for a moment to respond to a question from a teammate.

Marvin wondered what Luis meant by required training. He thought about how training had worked in his organization and in other organizations he'd seen. People were scheduled for training, then were pulled out by supervisors because of some bureaucratic crisis—the vice president was making a visit, or more people were needed to take inventory. Sandy Fitzwilliam was obviously a leader committed to training as a way to bring about needed change.

When Luis returned, Marvin asked him how many requests Sandy got to work people's shifts.

"Not one," Luis answered. "When top managers are squarely behind the training of teams, it really smooths the way. Remember, the second step to empowerment?"

"Clear boundaries lead to empowerment," said Marvin. "I see. But what about all the dissatisfaction and discouragement you said people were experiencing? How did they work through it?"

"It took a while," said Luis. "In our training we learned that groups, like individuals, go through predictable stages of development. They need different kinds of leadership at each stage."

"Tell me more about the group stages," Marvin said, once again getting out his notebook and pen.

"When a group first forms, members are typically enthusiastic, but they don't know how they're going to operate or who's going to play what role. That's called the *orientation stage*, and it's a time when a team needs strong, clear leadership. Someone has to set the agendas and organize the team's efforts.

"We didn't do that initially, and our teams quickly moved into the second stage of development, the *dissatisfaction stage*. The reality of working as a team always seems to be more difficult than team members expect. In the training sessions we learned that teams in dissatisfaction need continued strong, clear leadership. But they also need support— someone to listen to their concerns and cheerlead for any progress made. We learned that, while this dissatisfaction stage is uncomfortable, it's a critical stage for ultimately becoming a high-performing team. It was in this dissatisfaction stage that we began to experiment with a role we still use today called the 'team coordinator.'"

Marvin said, "We use team leaders in my company, but I have an idea you mean something a little different."

Luis nodded and said, "During the initial stages of our teams, the team coordinator, in many ways, acts like a manager. After a team moves into *resolution*— the third stage of team development, when members begin to learn to work together—we start to rotate the role of team coordinator among team members. The role of the coordinator is to support and facilitate the team.

"Also, it's important that team members understand what's going on in other areas," continued Luis, "So the coordinator attends weekly meetings of other departments and reports back to the team. This supports one of the organization's key values—cross-training and cross-utilization. Most of the decisions are made as a team, but the coordinator does the detail part, handling most of the paper work, scheduling people for vacation time, and so forth.

"The coordinator also trains the next person in rotation. We found that the team coordinator role becomes less critical as the final *production stage* of development is reached. A self-directed team acts to direct and support individual efforts itself. Again and again we learned the value of diversity as a real asset for dealing with the complex problems we face today. And when I talk about diversity I'm not just talking about race and sex but also cultural background, as well as ability and opinion. We found that by drawing upon the unique skills, perspectives and knowledge of our team members, we developed far better solutions to our problems."

"So as people's capabilities and contributions increase, the whole becomes greater than the sum of its parts," Marvin summarized. "But I know that dealing with diversity can be difficult. It's much easier if everyone thinks alike. Haven't there ever been times when your teams just blew it?"

"Oh, sure," replied Luis. "Many times teams have learned the hard way. They've failed to utilize their resources and explore differences of opinion and tried to railroad decisions through."

"What happened?"

"It backfired. Next time the team had to decide something, those members whose ideas were ignored were uncooperative."

"So team development really involves using a lot of human relations skills."

"Absolutely. Any time we're to make a decision on a complex matter, we have to make sure each person has an opportunity to express his or her opinions and concerns. We do this not only to be fair but so that each individual's talents can be brought to bear on the problem."

"When a team has reached the production stage, what is it able to do?" asked Marvin.

"Over the last year or so, our teams have taken on more and more important decisions. A number of teams are now at a point where they actually do all or many of the functions traditionally viewed as the job of management—such as hiring and disciplining, performance evaluations, allocation of resources, quality assurance. These teams have really replaced the old management hierarchy."

"Amazing!" exclaimed Marvin. He shook his head thoughtfully.

"What's wrong?" asked Luis.

"Several times today I've been faced with the evidence that empowerment really works, but it challenges my old beliefs."

"Hey, join the club," laughed Luis. "Most managers would say that if you trust people to be responsible for performing these functions and monitoring themselves, you're just asking for trouble. Maybe that would have been true of individuals the way they were accustomed to being treated under the old command-and-control management model. But when you empower people with information and boundaries and then train them to operate in self-directed teams, it's different.

"Since we started our journey to empowerment, I've come to see that people are an untapped resource. When they understand that you're trusting them to use their brains and their abilities, their own sense of responsibility kicks in. It's as if they've just been waiting for a chance to view the organization as their own, so they could improve it. Combine this intelligence and energy with a shared commitment to serving the customer, and you've got something really powerful!

"What's more," Luis continued, "we keep getting better and better, and people continue to grow and develop new skills and abilities."

"In fact, if people are not continuing to grow and develop, then we find that they just don't seem to fit here anymore, and they wind up leaving. As long as people want to continue to grow, continue to develop, and continue to stretch themselves, they have a place here—they really fit. And that means we wind up having an organization that is profitable in many ways.

"I've developed a list of all the benefits of self-directed teams:"

Benefits of Self-Directed Teams

• Increased job satisfaction

• Attitude change from "have to" to "want to"

• Greater employee commitment

• Better communication between employees and management

• More efficient decision-making process

• Improved quality

• Reduced operating costs

• More profitable organization

"And for all those payoffs to occur," replied Marvin, "your self-directed teams need to have a great deal of information. Now I understand further why information sharing was the first key to empowerment."

"You're absolutely right. And the need for information sharing continues to grow," explained Luis. "We have had to develop better mechanisms for recording information and for making it available to more people. One of the beauties of the new computer technology is that it allows us to put information into a form that's readily available to everyone through our PC networks. Everybody knows what's going on all the time. You see, for teams to be responsible, they demand a tremendous amount of information, more than they've ever had.

"We've also found as we've operated," Luis continued, "that our team members are asking for only the information that's really useful to them. That keeps us from being inundated with requests for information that they'll never use.

"That means we don't have to prepare as many reports as before, but the reports we do prepare convey important information to our teams. Since teams are thinking about the importance of what they do, they're continually looking for better ways to do things and more ways to utilize the skills and abilities they have. After all, this is their organization, isn't it?"

"Fascinating," said Marvin. "I'm finally getting a handle on how empowerment works and the impact it can have on organizational performance."

"Great! I'm glad I could help," smiled Luis.

Marvin thanked Luis and headed out thinking, I'll stop by Sandy's office and see if she has any final words of wisdom before I start—I mean restart—my journey to the Land of Empowerment.

$\mathbf{A}$s Marvin walked back to Sandy's office he was feeling good about all he had learned. It seemed like a long time ago when he had been dragging his feet.

"Well, are you ready to go?" Sandy smiled as she greeted him.

"I think so. Your associates have been very helpful, and I've learned a great deal about empowerment. Implementing the three keys sounds like a real challenge but also a great gift to everyone in our company."

"There is no doubt that you will need persistence in your belief that empowerment will work."

"Particularly with the last key—replacing the old hierarchy with self-directed teams," said Marvin. "Information sharing got me at first, but the role of teams seems even tougher."

"That's the part that always makes managers doubt the whole process," Sandy replied.

"When the confusion and dissatisfaction stage sets in, it must seem so out of control," Marvin said in a pained tone.

"Yes! Know why?" Sandy asked. "Because if you are going to be held accountable, you want to be in control."

"Right!"

"But the reality is that if you're going to empower people, you have to give up control and still remain accountable."

"Very scary for a manager."

"Especially when the organization gets to this stage of confusion and lack of leadership regarding next steps."

"The training sounds like it helps," said Marvin. "Just knowing that dissatisfaction is a natural, predictable stage of group development probably puts things in perspective."

"That's why I required the training," Sandy said. "I had tried before to empower people but didn't know the inevitability or severity of the dissatisfaction stage. When confusion and disillusionment began to occur, I was as scared as anyone. I was afraid I'd created a monster that none of us would be able to control. I wanted to head for the hills and abdicate."

"But you didn't, obviously."

"No, but I've seen a lot of managers do just that, and empowerment often goes by the wayside."

"How did you hang in there?"

"Naive enthusiasm, probably," she laughed. "I kept reminding myself and everyone else that people really did want to be empowered, and it could make a performance difference in our organization. But I want to tell you, many a night I sat at my desk staring into space and wondering what I had gotten myself into. The Land of Empowerment seemed far away. I sensed a leadership vacuum in the organization. Here I was asking people to make a major change in their way of relating to each other, but neither I nor the other managers knew what guidance to provide. It was a very frustrating period for everyone."

"What happened?" quizzed Marvin.

"Gradually something interesting began to happen. It's like in the movies when the hero is on his last leg and you can't figure out how he's going to make it."

"But he always does!"

"Sure. That's what makes a good movie. The solution comes from some source you hadn't expected. That's what happened in our empowerment experience. Right in the midst of the leadership vacuum, flickering lights of empowerment began to shine from colleagues on the teams. Teams began to make important action decisions, individuals risked speaking out with suggestions, and managers acted like facilitators."

"Out of the discomfort of the leadership vacuum, the very empowerment we wanted was born. The information sharing, new boundaries, and skills training for teams began to pay off."

"I don't know if I could have hung in there," reflected Marvin.

"That's why it's important to understand that the empowerment journey begins with direction during the orientation stage and requires you to add support to your efforts as natural dissatisfaction sets in. Any wavering from the vision at that time could be disastrous."

"So staying in the middle of the fray can speed up the movement to self-directed teams, even when you are unsure what to do to help?"

"That's it," Sandy said. "When it seems no one has the answer, people come forward in ways that can astonish you. And you can naturally become a facilitator who eventually becomes a group member."

"The key seems to be to stick to your beliefs," said Marvin as he wrote some thoughts in his notebook.

That's the only way your beliefs can become reality, but sometimes it can be very scary."

"Well, you said in the beginning that the journey to the Land of Empowerment would not be easy," said Marvin. "I understand that thoroughly now, but I'm still ready to go."

"Good luck," Sandy said as they walked to the door.

"I'll need it," said Marvin. "And you'll be hearing from me."

"Any time," Sandy replied as she waved good-bye to him. "And remember," she added, "it does work—if you stick with it."

Marvin spent that evening collecting his thoughts and preparing to begin the empowerment journey with his organization.

He spent a good deal of time arranging and rearranging a set of cards on which he had transferred all his notes.

Finally, he came up with something he called the *Empowerment Game Plan.* This game plan summarized the three keys to empowerment and used arrows to show the interplay that is needed among all three. He decided he would give copies to everyone in his organization. It looked like this:

THE EMPOWERMENT GAME PLAN

Start with—

Sharing Information with Everyone

- Share performance information about the company; help people understand the business.
- Build trust through sharing.
- Set up self-monitoring possibilities.
- View mistakes as learning opportunities.
- Break down hierarchical thinking; help people behave as owners.

Then

And

Create Autonomy through Boundaries

- Clarify the big and little pictures.

- Clarify goals and roles.

- Define values and rules that underlie actions.

- Create rules and procedures that support empowerment.

- Provide needed training.

- Hold people accountable for results.

Replace the Old Hierarchy with Self-Directed Teams

- Provide direction and skills training for empowered teams.

- Provide support and encouragement for change.

- Use diversity as a team asset.

- Gradually give control to the teams.

- Recognize there will be some tough times.

Over the next few months, Marvin and his company traveled along their own unique journey toward the Land of Empowerment. At first, he made periodic calls to Sandy Fitzwilliam for advice and feedback. Over time, however, as his confidence grew, he and his associates became engaged in their own process of developing an empowered organization. Despite occasional setbacks, they persisted, and eventually they achieved their goal.

Just as Sandy had acted as a guide for Marvin, he found himself counseling other executives who were moving through their own journeys. Again and again he heard himself say,

"Empowerment
isn't magic.

It consists
of a few simple steps
and a lot of persistence."

* * *

Acknowledgments

There are so many people to thank and acknowledge for the learnings that led to this book. Inevitably, we will leave out some people, but we will do our best to be as complete as possible. In order to cover as many bases as possible (without writing another book), we offer "thank you's" to a special group of people who have been most helpful in the formulation of our ideas. We also offer acknowledgments to a much wider list of people and companies we have learned from as they reacted to earlier drafts of our book. To all, we wish to express our sincerest appreciation. We know they will recognize their contributions throughout the book.

Thank you to the following companies and people in them who have been courageous in their pioneering efforts to empower people and organizations:

Mary Andrulewicz, Jack Kent and all the business unit leaders at Sheppard-Pratt Hospital

George Clifton (retired) and many others in the East Bay Region of Pacific Gas and Electric Company

Ron Floto, Dennis Carter, Lewis Payne, the top management team and the many district and store managers at Kash 'N' Karry Stores

Jeanne Gruner and the Performance Management Task Force at Household International

Tom Jackson, Mike Squilante, Jeff Beck, and a host of others from Advanta Corporation

Lanny Julian and the amazing field staff of Ambassador Cards

David Liddle of Circle K Stores (U.K.)

Jim Pantelidas, Ron McIntosh, Gordon Olitch, and Wolfgang Greogry of Petro-Canada

Irv Rule and Matthew Reimann of Seimens Medical Systems, plus John Donnelly, formerly of Siemens Medical Systems

Ralph Stayer of Johnsonville Foods for showing us and many others the way to create real empowerment

Steve Wachter and the managers and employees of General Electric Information Services

George Wilson and many others at Florida Power and Light, plus Jo-Anne Pitera and Barbara Dabney, formerly at Florida Power and Light

Acknowledgments to the following people who read earlier drafts of the book and shared openly of their experiences in giving us feedback on the book:

Barbara Balter with the Robert B. Balter Company

Joe Bode with Black and Decker Corporation

Don J. Carlos and Bill Carlos, brothers emeritus

Arnie Cole with the U.S. Army

John Coleman with CSX Corporation

Bruce Dalgleish with General Mills Restaurants

Mike Gill with Americom Cellular

Charles J. Loew with Motorola University

Mike Louden with Louden Associates

Rick Miller with the Boys and Girls Club of Phoenix

Mike Perry with the E. I. Du Pont Company

Al Price with the Mauna Kea Beach Hotel

Joe Raymond with the Georgia Academy

Lou Reymann formerly with Shimadzu Scientific
Instruments

Al Schneider with the Federal Communications
Commission

Julie Seeherman with Venture Stores

Tom Walczykowski with the FBI

We would like to express our sincere thanks to
Carlita Anthony-Mines, Valerie Hall, Michele Jansen,
Harry Paul, and Eleanor Terndrup, for producing
this book in a most efficient manner and to Bob
Nelson for his helpful feedback and editing.

We would also like to thank Margret McBride, our
agent, and Steven Piersanti, editor at Berrett-
Koehler, for their encouragement and energy in
publishing this book.

In addition, we owe an intellectual debt to many of our colleagues at Blanchard Training and Development, especially Eunice Parisi-Carew and Don Carew for sharing their knowledge about team development; Jesse Stoner and Drea Zigarmi for their thinking about creating a compelling vision; Pat Zigarmi for new insights on Situational Leadership® II; and Dev Ogle for sharing his knowledge of continuous improvement and strategic thinking.

Most importantly, we would like to thank our wives— Marjorie Blanchard, Lynne Carlos, and Ruth Anne Randolph—whose support and challenging questions helped us refine this book to a high level of value for our readers.

Ken Blanchard would also like to acknowledge the impact a visit with C. O. Woody, Rita Craig, and some of the good folks from the Power Generation Business Unit of Florida Power and Light had on his thinking about self-directed teams. In particular, a big One Minute Praising goes to Rick Beil, Eddie Childs, Mary Polk, and Debra Shultz-Robinson, who have been involved in self-directed teams at the Turkey Point Fossil and Cutler Plants. Their experience has been heartwarming and successful.

John Carlos would also like to praise

Mike Vance—my phantom mentor for over twenty years

Rick and Ester Miller—for standing by me when many didn't

Lino and Kelly Antunes, Andee and Todd Oleno— my children, who have always been an inspiration

Gordon Dolan—a good friend and colleague

First Sergeant Harold J. Merton—who first taught me about leadership

Alan Randolph would also like to praise

Barry Posner and Jackie Schmidt-Posner for their constant friendship and colleagueship

Dan Costello for his support and encouragement

Father Vincent Dwyer for his early inspiration

My children—Ashley, Shannon and Liza, who inspire me to be empowered and to empower them

About the Authors

Ken Blanchard has had tremendous impact on the day-to-day management of people and companies.

As a writer in the field of management, his impact has been far-reaching. His One Minute Manager Library, which includes *The One Minute Manager®* (1982), *Putting the One Minute Manager to Work* (1984), *Leadership and the One Minute Manager* (1985), *The One Minute Manager Gets Fit* (1986), *The One Minute Manager Meets the Monkey* (1989), and *The One Minute Manager Builds High Performing Teams* (1990), has collectively sold more than seven million copies and has been translated into more than twenty languages.

Ken has also coauthored several books: *Management of Organizational Behavior* (with Dr. Paul Hersey), a classic textbook now in its sixth edition; *The Power of Ethical Management* (1988, with Dr. Norman Vincent Peale); *Raving Fans: A Revolutionary Approach to Customer Service* (1992, with Sheldon Bowles); and his most recent book, *Everyone's a Coach* (1995, with Don Shula). *We Are the Beloved* (1994), highlights Ken's spiritual journey.

Ken is chairman of Blanchard Training and Development, a full-service management consulting and training company that he founded in 1979 with his wife, Marjorie Blanchard. He maintains a visiting lectureship at Cornell University, where he also serves as Trustee Emeritus. The Blanchards live in San Diego.

John P. Carlos is a highly skilled management consultant, trainer, and motivational speaker.

With twenty-five years of hands-on experience as a manager and trainer, his knowledge of organizational and management development, succession planning, team empowerment, customer service, leadership training, and managing diversity is considered to be at the leading edge of today's technology. John specializes in organization and people development, empowering teams, and developing companies to deliver legendary customer service.

As a speaker, he is best known for his humorous and insightful real-life stories and his ability to focus people on their own behavior. His years of experience include private, for profit, and nonprofit organizations, convenience stores, hotels and resorts, and residential treatment schools for adjudicated, hard-to-place teenagers. For ten years he was the director of training for Circle K, a retail food company with over five thousand outlets worldwide. He heads his own consulting group and is a senior associate with Blanchard Training and Development.

John received a bachelor's degree in business and an M.B.A. from Columbia Pacific University. He now lives with his wife, Lynne Carlos, in Phoenix, Arizona. His two grown daughters, Kelly and Andee, and his sons-in-law, Todd and Lino, also live in Arizona.

Alan Randolph is an internationally respected and highly accomplished management educator and consultant.

Alan has consulted on management and organizational skills and issues with domestic and international organizations in both public and private sectors, for the last twenty years. His specialties include empowerment, project planning and management, performance management, leadership, customer service, and team building. As a seminar presenter and speaker, he is relaxed, clear, and to the point.

Alan is professor of management at the University of Baltimore's Merrick School of Business and a senior associate with Blanchard Training and Development. He has published a variety of articles in both practitioner and academic journals. He is coauthor of *Getting the Job Done: Managing Project Teams and Task Forces for Success* (1992, with Barry Posner) and of *The Organization Game* (1993, with Robert Miles and Edward Kemery).

Alan holds a bachelor's degree in industrial engineering from Georgia Institute of Technology, a master's degree in personnel and industrial relations, and a Ph.D. degree in business administration from the University of Massachusetts, Amherst.

He and his wife, Ruth Anne Randolph (also a senior associate with Blanchard Training and Development), and their daughters, Ashley, Shannon, and Liza, live in Baltimore, Maryland.

Services Available

Blanchard Training and Development (BTD) is a full-service consulting and training company in the areas of empowerment, leadership, teamwork, performance management, customer service, quality management, ethics, and visioning.

Empowerment is the latest in a long line of key leadership concepts that BTD has made easy to understand and accessible to managers in both the private and public sectors. Based upon research and consultation with a wide variety of companies since the mid 1980s, the empowerment concepts have been developed to assist managers in guiding their people and organizations to the Land of Empowerment. The keys to empowerment make significant links to many other topics that have been developed by BTD: Situational Leadership® II; Building High Performing Teams; Creating Your Organization's Future; Total Quality Leadership; Situational Self Leadership; and Partnering for Performance Management.

BTD offers consulting, training, and speaking services and a complete product line of videos and print material designed to enhance individual and organizational learning and change.

To learn more about how BTD can help empower your people and organization, please call or write:

Blanchard Training and Development, Inc.
125 State Place
Escondido, CA 92029
800-728-6000 or 619-489-5005

You may contact Ken Blanchard and John Carlos directly through the BTD office in Escondido at the above numbers. You may contact Alan Randolph directly at the BTD office in Baltimore at 410-321-8231.

The authors are also available on-line through PRODIGY at DMVT33A or CompuSERV at 76121,1545 and/or 74563,1527.

An Invitation

In our quest for continued learning about empowerment and the journey to get there, we invite you to send us stories describing your experiences and insights about empowerment. Send your comments to

The Empowerment File
Ken Blanchard, John Carlos, and Alan Randolph
Blanchard Training and Development, Inc.
125 State Place
Escondido, CA 92029